Caught Reading PLUS

Getting Ready Teacher's Manual

Program Consultant
Teri Swanson, Ph.D.
Sweetwater Union High School District
San Diego, California

GLOBE FEARON
Pearson Learning Group

Getting Ready **Program Consultant:** Teri Swanson, Ph.D.

Dr. Teri Swanson holds a Ph.D. from Wichita State University, Kansas. Her area of expertise includes the effect of phonemic awareness on literacy acquisition. She has been a speech pathologist for the past 27 years. Since 1987, she has also been in charge of reading programs for students with phonemic awareness deficiencies in the Sweetwater School District in San Diego, California.

Teacher Reviewers:

Colleen Arnold
Special Educator
Morningside Elementary School
Atlanta, Georgia

Kathryn Mackie
Special Educator
Riverside Middle School
Dearborn Heights, Michigan

Robert Fass
Reading Resource Room Teacher
Martin Luther King, Jr. Junior High School
North Sacramento, California

Ray Pedraza
ESL Teacher
Southwest Middle School
Reading, Pennsylvania

Program Developers: Becky Manfredini, Jenny Della Penna

Project Editor: Brian Hawkes

Assistant Editor: Gina Dalessio

Editorial Assistants: Jennifer Keezer, Jenna Thorsland

Designer: Jennifer Sabino

Production Editor: Regina McAloney

Electronic Page Production: Debbie Childers, Leslie Greenberg, Phyllis Rosinsky, Jeffrey Engel

Cover Design: Sharon Ferguson

ISBN 0-130-23338-2
Printed in the United States of America
5 6 7 8 9   07 06 05 04 03

1-800-321-3106
www.pearsonlearning.com

CONTENTS

Welcome to the *Getting Ready* components of the *Caught Reading Plus* program! *Getting Ready* is designed to provide all of the basics of literacy instruction in an appropriate and engaging way for the older student.

Components of *Getting Ready*

Getting Ready consists of a Teacher's Manual and Worktext that cover:

- **phonemic awareness**
- **basic phonics**
- **the alphabetic principle**

The Teacher's Manual includes a variety of opportunities for informal assessment and reteaching activities. As a convenience for teachers, tear-out token cards and letter cards are provided in the back of the book.

The Worktext includes engaging activities and short reading passages covering a variety of genres. The pages are designed to spark and hold students' interest.

Why Teach Phonemic Awareness?

Phonemic awareness is the understanding that words are composed of various combinations of the sounds (or phonemes) of a language. Phonemic awareness is an insight about oral language and is a necessary prerequisite for beginning reading instruction.

Recent research has shown that approximately 25 percent of all students will not develop phonemic awareness on their own through normal reading instruction. Without explicit instruction, these students are at risk for becoming poor readers. These students and, in fact, all students can benefit from explicit phonemic awareness instruction as presented here in the *Getting Ready* program.

How Does Phonemic Awareness Relate to Phonics?

Understanding that running speech can be segmented into sounds is a critical step in learning to read and write an alphabetic language. The alphabet is, in fact, a code that assigns letters to the various phonemes of the language in a relatively consistent manner. Students must understand the idea behind the code (phonemic awareness) before they can begin to master it (phonics) and become literate.

Phonics instruction involves explicitly teaching the letter-sound correspondences. Learning this "code" is essential for students to begin to **decode** text (the first steps to reading) as well as **encode** text (spelling and writing).

Chapter Content

The *Getting Ready* program is organized into seven chapters.

- **Chapter 1:** alphabet
- **Chapters 2–4:** three-sound words
- **Chapter 5:** four-sound words
- **Chapter 6:** five- and six-sound words
- **Chapter 7:** multisyllabic words

Consistent, Straightforward Instruction

Within each chapter, the presentation is consistent through all five lessons.

Token Lesson A The two token lessons in each chapter provide teacher-directed instruction (there is no corresponding lesson in the Worktext). Teachers use the tear-out token cards from the back of the Teacher's Manual and a bank of nonsense words to help students develop phonemic awareness. Because tokens and nonsense words are used, students cannot rely on letter shapes or their visual memory. All nonsense words are "new" and must be decoded.

Token Lesson B In Token Lesson B, students continue to work with token cards and transition to letter cards. They begin to connect sounds to letters, developing the basic phonics skills. They also work on blending sounds. Chapters 1 and 7 do not have token lessons.

Lesson 1 Students learn spelling rules and the conventions of written English. There are accompanying activities in the Worktext for students to try out what they have learned.

Lesson 2 Students begin working with banks of real words and letter cards. They can also use the game-based activities in their Worktexts to develop and reinforce their skills.

Lesson 3 Students have an opportunity to practice their decoding skills by reading short selections in a variety of genres. Their reading is followed by a writing exercise, where they can practice their encoding skills.

Assessment and Reteaching

- **Informal Assessments** in every chapter help track students' progress.
- **Reteaching** suggestions included in Teacher Tip boxes provide additional techniques for student success.
- **Final Assessment** helps teachers determine when students are ready to move on to *Caught Reading Plus*, Level 1.

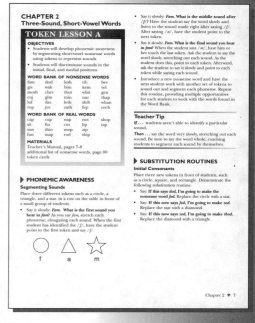

	1	2	3	4	5	6	7
Phonemic Awareness		✓	✓	✓	✓	✓	✓
Alphabetic Principle	✓						
Visual Discrimination	✓						
Auditory Discrimination	✓						
Letter Recognition	✓						
Short Vowels	✓	✓					
Long Vowels	✓		✓				
Consonant Digraphs	✓						
Double Consonants		✓				✓	
Vowel Digraphs	✓						
Dipthongs	✓		✓		✓		
Initial Consonants		✓	✓				
Final Consonants		✓	✓				
Medial Consonants		✓	✓				
Syllabification			✓				✓
Vowel Pairs	✓		✓				
Silent Letters			✓		✓		
Homophones			✓				
Y as a Vowel				✓			
Soft and Hard *c* and *g*				✓			
Consonant Blends				✓	✓	✓	
r-Controlled Vowels					✓		
Inflectional Endings						✓	
Compound Words							✓
Suffixes						✓	✓
Prefixes							✓
Reading Strategies		✓	✓	✓	✓	✓	✓
Writing Skills		✓	✓	✓	✓	✓	✓
Spelling		✓	✓	✓	✓	✓	✓
Listening Skills	✓	✓	✓	✓	✓	✓	✓

CHAPTER 1
Tools for *Getting Ready*

LESSON 1

OBJECTIVES
- Students will recognize that the upper and lower case letters of the alphabet represent vowel sounds and consonants
- Students will match consonant sounds to corresponding letters
- Students will identify consonants that can make two sounds

WORD BANK OF WORDS
CONTAINING *c, g, s, x*

pencil	game	nose	xylophone
cake	garage	serious	Xerox
coffee	dragon	please	fax
circle	gentle	sit	box
cycle	gauge	sock	six

MATERIALS
Worktext, page 5
Teacher's Manual, pages 1–2
letter cards from A to Z

Teacher Tip

It may be surprising to find that some students may not have complete phonics or alphabetic knowledge. They may not have correctly associated specific letters to sounds. Before moving into Chapter 2, which focuses on three-sound words, it will be important for students to have a basic knowledge of the alphabet and the sounds each letter or combinations of letters make. You may wish to use this chapter as a reference tool while your students work through Chapters 2–7.

▶ THE ALPHABET

Sounds and Letters, From A to Z

- Provide each student with a shuffled set of letter cards, from A to Z. Ask them to organize the cards in alphabetical order.
- As you see each student complete the task, ask the student to point to each letter card, beginning with A, and name the letter. Make a checklist to keep track of students who don't have complete alphabetic knowledge and need additional work with specific sounds and letters.

Categories, From A to Z

- Make columns of words for each letter of the alphabet. Invite students to put their first names under the correct category, such as *Mm* for *Maya*, or *Jj* for *Joseph*. Have them complete the same routine with their last names, such as *Oo* for *Ortiz*. Rotating around the room, ask students to add their favorite words under the correct category.
- Brainstorm these words by encouraging students to think of their favorite sports, activities, and foods. Have them also look around the room and find objects in the room that they can add to the columns. As students progress through *Getting Ready*, have them continue adding words they've decoded and can read.

▶ CONSONANTS

One-Sound Consonants

Distribute photocopies of the alphabet. Tell students that you want to focus on the consonants first. Invite students to circle all of the consonants in the alphabet. Explain that most consonants make one sound, but some can make two sounds, such as *c, g, s,* and *x*. Save those consonants for later and begin by having students name the others and say each sound.

Teacher Tip

As students say the sound that each letter makes, coach them to say each sound without an *uh* at the end of it. For example, *Bb* is /*b*/, not *buh*. *Zz* is *zzzzz*, not *zuh*. The stop consonants such as /*b*/ or /*d*/ will be more difficult to say without the *uh*. Encourage students to say them as short as possible. By not adding a vowel sound at the end, students will be less confused when they begin segmenting and decoding three-sound words, such as *bit*. Instead of /*bu*//*i*//*tuh*/, they will segment and decode it correctly: /*b*/ /*i*/ /*t*/.

Alliterative Tongue Twisters

- Working with consonants that make one sound, have students brainstorm funny tongue twisters, such as *Dan Dougherty drives a Dodge to Dartmouth, eating donuts with Dalia Darling and her dogs, Diggy and Dougie.*
- Encourage students to use the dictionary to create their tongue twisters.

Two-Sound Consonants

- Write the following categories on the board:

Cc	Gg	Ss	Xx
/k/ /s/	/g/ /j/	/s/ /z/	/ks/ /z/

  Mention to students that some consonants make more than one sound. Begin working with words in the Word Bank that contain the letter c. Since students may not be able to decode the words, point to the following words and say each one, having students echo you: **pencil**, **cake**, **coffee**, **circle**, **cycle**. Next, invite students to put each word under the correct category. Explain that some of the words have a hard sound like /k/, while other words have a soft sound, like /s/. Ask them if any words contain both sounds. (*circle, cycle*)

- Now have students work with hard and soft *g*, repeating the same routine with words from the Word Bank. In Chapter 4, students will be completing spelling exercises on both hard and soft *c* and *g*. (Worktext pages 26–27)

- Complete the other categories on the board for *s* and *x*, using words from the Word Bank.

▶ **PRACTICE**

Favorite Words

Have students complete Worktext page 5, having them associate and list a favorite word for each letter of the alphabet.

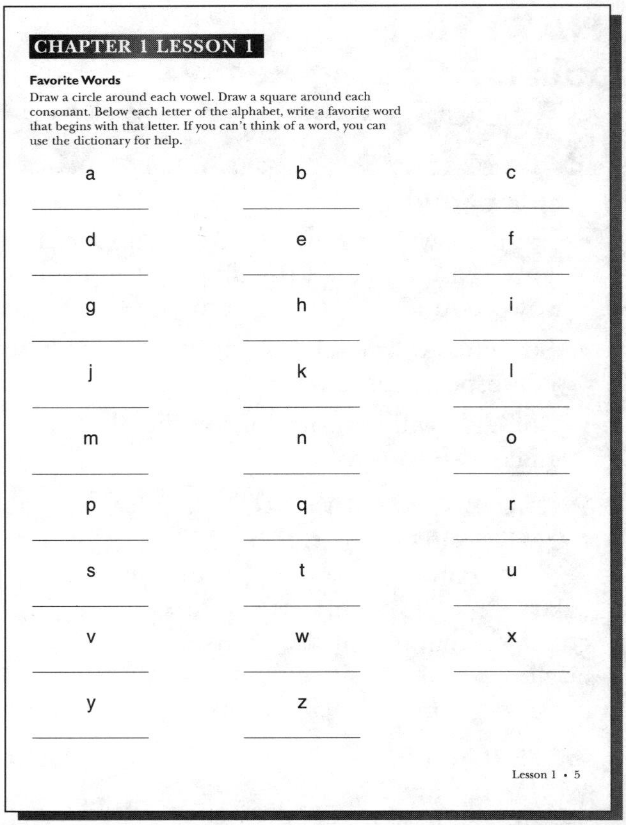

CHAPTER 1 LESSON 1

Favorite Words

Draw a circle around each vowel. Draw a square around each consonant. Below each letter of the alphabet, write a favorite word that begins with that letter. If you can't think of a word, you can use the dictionary for help.

a	b	c
d	e	f
g	h	i
j	k	l
m	n	o
p	q	r
s	t	u
v	w	x
y	z	

Lesson 1 • 5

Worktext page 5

LESSON 2

OBJECTIVES
- Students will recognize that consonant digraphs such as *ch*, *sh*, *th*, and *wh* represent one sound
- Students will identify words containing consonant digraphs

WORD BANK OF WORDS CONTAINING CONSONANT DIGRAPHS

sheep	chill	thing	white
shake	cheer	thick	wheat
shy	chop	think	whale
shed	cheese	that	while
shin	chat	then	when

MATERIALS
Worktext, page 6
Teacher's Manual, page 3
letter cards and consonant digraph cards, *ch, sh, th, wh*

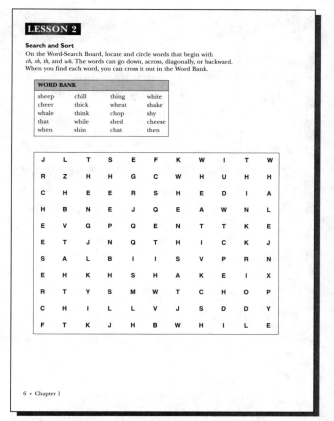

Worktext page 6

▶ CONSONANT DIGRAPHS

Sorting Sounds

Write the following categories on the board: **ch**, **sh**, **th**, **wh**. Point to and say each sound, having students echo you. Then say the word **sheep**, elongating and stretching the initial consonant digraph. Ask a volunteer to name the category it belongs to, writing the word underneath it. Do the same routine with the words *chill*, *thing*, and *white*.

Rhyming Sounds

Say the word **hill**. Ask students to think of a word that rhymes with *hill* and begins with *ch*. (*chill*) Then write the word under that category. Do the same routine with the following words: *bake/shake*; *pop/chop*; *pick/thick*; *bite/white*.

▶ PRACTICE

Search and Sort

Have students turn to page 6 in the Worktext. Have them find hidden words on the Word-Search Board and circle them. Then ask them to sort the words according to each initial consonant digraph.

LESSON 3

OBJECTIVES

- Students will recognize that long vowels make the same sound as their letter name
- Students will identify long-vowel words with the spelling pattern vowel-consonant-*e*, as well as vowel pairs *ai*, *ay*, *ee*, *ea*, *ie*, *oa*, and *ow*

WORD BANK OF LONG-VOWEL WORDS

game	need	bike	cove	tune
main	deep	tie	row	mule
day	meal	kite	boat	June
rain	each	pie	soap	cute

MATERIALS

Worktext, page 7
Teacher's Manual, page 4
letter cards

▶ LONG VOWELS

Distribute photocopies of the alphabet. Ask students to circle the letters that represent vowel sounds. Mention to students that long vowels make the same sound as their letter names. For example, long *a* sounds like /*a*/ in *ate*; long *e* sounds like /*e*/ in *eat*; long *i* sounds like /*i*/ in *ice*; long *o* sounds like /*o*/ in *open*; and long *u* sounds like /*u*/ in *uniform*.

Sorting Sounds

Write the following categories on the board: **long a**, **long e**, **long i**, **long o**, **long u**. Explain to students that long-vowel words can be spelled vowel-consonant-*e*, as in *bake*, *Pete*, *hike*, *hope*, *cube*. Write the words under the correct categories. Mention that in a vowel pair where two vowels are next to each other, the first vowel says its name, while the second one is silent, as in *stain*, *lie*, *reach*, and *coat*. Also explain that *ay*, when it is at the end of a word, usually sounds like long *a*, as in *hay*. Add these words to the categories. Coach students in brainstorming words that contain long vowels, and have volunteers sound out and write these words on the board.

Rhyming Sounds

Provide a set of letter cards to pairs of students. Have them build the word *game*. Then ask them to make the word *came*, substituting the initial consonant to form a new long *a* word. Then ask them to make the words *fame*, *name*, *same*, and *tame*. Use other words in the Word Bank to have students build other long-vowel and rhyming words.

▶ PRACTICE

Fill in the Blanks

Have students turn to page 7 in their Worktexts. Using their Word Bank as a reference, have them fill in the blanks to create long-vowel words. You may wish to have students work in pairs for this activity. Rotating around the room, help students decode and read the words. Keep a checklist handy to record whether students are able to sound out a consonant or vowel.

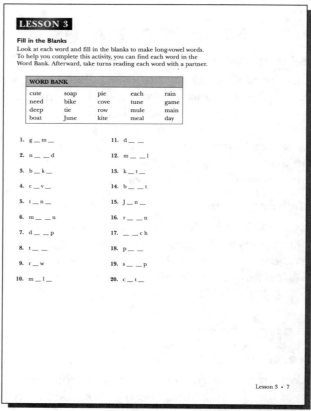

Worktext page 7

LESSON 4

OBJECTIVES
- Students will recognize the sounds made by short vowels
- Students will identify words containing short vowels
- Students will sort words containing short vowels

WORD BANK OF SHORT-VOWEL WORDS

at	Ed	it	on	up
am	hen	in	cot	us
an	beg	if	log	tub
tap	get	sip	mop	bug

MATERIALS
Worktext, page 8
Teacher's Manual, page 5

▶ SHORT VOWELS

- Say the following word slowly: **at**. Ask students to say it slowly. Then have them say it again, but ask them to stop before they get to the last part of the word. By cutting the word in half, they have accessed and emphasized the short-vowel sound. Repeat this routine with other short-vowel words, such as *Ed, it, on, up.*

- For students who speak English as a second language, you may want to use the word *off* instead of *on.*

Teacher Tip
You may want to present the short-vowel sounds in a sequence such as /a/, /e/, /i/, /o/, and /u/, placing contrasting vowel sounds next to each other so that students are able to discriminate sounds more easily.

Sorting Short-Vowel Words
- Write the following categories on the board: **short a**, **short e**, **short i**, **short o**, **short u**. Have students brainstorm 25 short-vowel words (5 of each short vowel) and write them underneath the correct categories.

- Using index cards, write each of the words. Afterward, have students take turns reading each word and saying the short-vowel sound. Shuffle the cards again, and have them sort each word according to its vowel sound. Invite them to think of other words for this flash-card and sorting routine.

▶ PRACTICE

A. Sort by Sound
Ask students to turn to page 8 in their Worktexts. Have them sort the words found in the Word Bank according to their short-vowel sounds.

B. Fill in the Blanks
Invite students to "Fill in the Blanks" by making short-vowel words. Have them check to see if they've made real words by using the dictionary.

LESSON 4

A. Sort by Sound
Look at each word found in the Word Bank. Look at the short vowel in each word and say it. Then sort each word according to its short-vowel sound. When you are finished, take turns reading the words with a partner.

WORD BANK				
it	Ed	on	up	at
us	cot	hen	in	am
tub	an	if	beg	log
mop	bug	get	tap	sip

short a	short e	short i	short o	short u
_____	_____	_____	_____	_____
_____	_____	_____	_____	_____
_____	_____	_____	_____	_____

B. Fill in the Blanks
Look at the words. There is a blank in the middle of the word. Fill in the blank with a vowel that will make a real word. Use a dictionary to check to see if you are making real words. Some of these words can use more than one vowel, such as: **c __ p   cap   cop   cup**.

1. p __ n   _____
2. t __ g   _____
3. m __ t   _____
4. b __ t   _____
5. f __ n   _____
6. n __ d   _____
7. r __ n   _____
8. s __ p   _____
9. v __ n   _____
10. t __ b   _____

8 • Chapter 1

Worktext page 8

LESSON 5

OBJECTIVES

- Students will recognize that diphthongs are comprised of two letters that make up one sound, such as the sound of /ou/ and /ow/ in *cloud* and *bow*, or the sound of /oi/ and /oy/ in *coin* and *toy*
- Students will identify words containing diphthongs
- Students will recognize that vowel digraphs /au/ and /aw/ usually have the same sound, as in *haul* and *paw*
- Students will identify words containing vowel digraphs

WORD BANK FOR WORDS WITH DIPHTHONGS AND VOWEL DIGRAPHS

cloud	bow	coin	toy	haul
paw	house	crown	oil	boy
Paul	crawl	mouth	flower	noise
joy	pause	yawn		

MATERIALS

Worktext, page 9
Teacher's Manual, page 6

▶ DIPHTHONGS AND VOWEL DIGRAPHS

- Write the following categories on the board: **ou–ow, oi–oy, au–aw**. Tell students that sometimes two letters can make one special sound that isn't a short-vowel or long-vowel sound. Say each of the above sounds and have students echo you. Then write a word from the Word Bank that matches each category, such as *house, crown, oil, toy, pause,* and *paw*. Invite students to say each word after you.

- Ask students to think of a rhyming word for each of the above words and include them under the correct categories.

▶ PRACTICE

A. Sort by Sound and Spelling Pattern

Have students open their Worktexts to page 9. Using the Word Bank, ask them to sort words according to their sound and spelling pattern.

B. Fill in the Blanks

Invite students to "Fill in the Blanks" to make words, using the Word Bank to check their spellings.

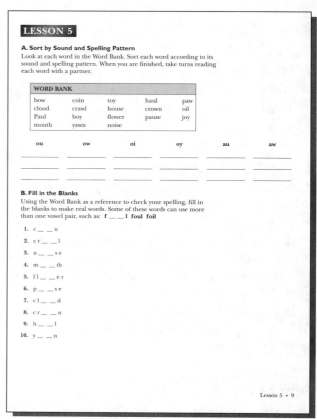

Worktext page 9

CHAPTER 2
Three-Sound, Short-Vowel Words

TOKEN LESSON A

OBJECTIVES
- Students will develop phonemic awareness by segmenting short-vowel nonsense words using tokens to represent sounds
- Students will discriminate sounds in the initial, final, and medial positions

WORD BANK OF NONSENSE WORDS

fam	dod	lesh	tib	bev
gis	wak	bim	kem	vel
mosh	chev	thut	whit	gen
cuj	gim	min	naz	thap
luf	daz	leth	shib	whan
rop	juv	zath	fep	roch

WORD BANK OF REAL WORDS

cap	cup	nap	not	shop
sit	fin	cut	lip	tap
sun	thin	mop	zip	
fun	map	rod	ship	

MATERIALS
Teacher's Manual, pages 7–8
additional list of nonsense words, page 72
token cards

▶ PHONEMIC AWARENESS

Segmenting Sounds

Place three different tokens such as a circle, a triangle, and a star in a row on the table in front of a small group of students.

- Say it slowly: *Fam.* **What is the first sound you hear in** *fam*? As you say *fam*, stretch each phoneme, elongating each sound. When the first student has identified the /f/, have the student point to the first token and say /f/.

f   a   m

- Say it slowly: *Fam.* **What is the middle sound after /f/?** Have the student say the word slowly and listen to the sound made right after saying /f/. After saying /a/, have the student point to the next token.

- Say it slowly: *Fam.* **What is the final sound you hear in** *fam*? When the student says /m/, have him or her touch the last token. Ask the student to say the word slowly, stretching out each sound. As the student does this, point to each token. Afterward, ask the student to say it slowly and point to each token while saying each sound.

- Introduce a new nonsense word and have the next student work with another set of tokens to sound out and segment each phoneme. Repeat this routine, providing multiple opportunities for each student to work with the words found in the Word Bank.

Teacher Tip

If . . . students aren't able to identify a particular sound,

Then . . . say the word very slowly, stretching out each sound. Be sure to say the word whole, coaching students to segment each sound by themselves.

▶ SUBSTITUTION ROUTINES

Initial Consonants

Place three new tokens in front of students, such as a circle, square, and rectangle. Demonstrate the following substitution routine.

- Say: **If this says** *dod*, **I'm going to make the nonsense word** *fod*. Replace the circle with a star.

- Say: **If this now says** *fod*, **I'm going to make** *zod*. Replace the star with a diamond.

- Say: **If this now says** *zod*, **I'm going to make** *thod*. Replace the diamond with a triangle.

- After modeling the previous routine, have students take turns substituting the initial sound. Work with three new tokens and say: **If this says** *lesh*, **make** *pesh*. **If this says** *pesh*, **make** *nesh*.

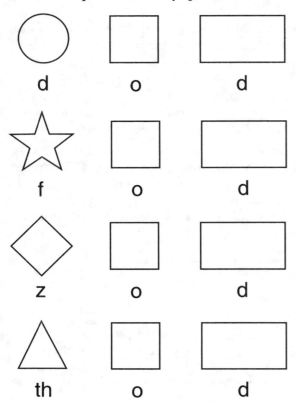

Medial Vowel Sounds

Place a square, triangle, and circle on the table.

- Say: **If this says** *bev*, **make** *biv*. Have a student replace the triangle with another token. Coach the student in substituting the medial vowel sound to make other nonsense words, such as *bov* and *bav*.

- As you have students continue to work with manipulating and substituting sounds in the initial, final, and medial positions, you may want to use additional short-vowel nonsense words found on page 72.

- After students have worked with short-vowel nonsense words, you can use the Word Bank of Real Words with them.

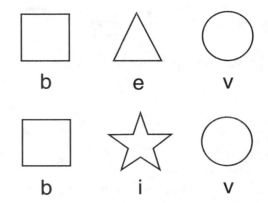

Final Consonants

Place a star, diamond, and rectangle in front of students.

- Say: **If this says** *tib*, **make** *tiz*. Have a student replace the rectangle with another token. Guide the student in substituting the final consonant sound to make *tid* and *tiv*.

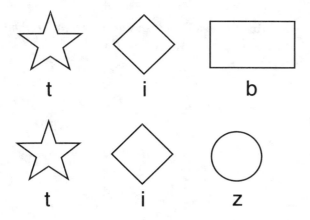

TOKEN LESSON B

OBJECTIVES
- Students will segment three-sound, short-vowel nonsense words by connecting sounds to letters
- Students will make new nonsense words by substituting beginning, final, and medial sounds and letters

WORD BANK OF NONSENSE WORDS

List 1	List 2	List 3	List 4
meb	rop	bam	pid
feb	sop	gam	fid
cheb	fop	nam	nid
chez	foz	nad	nith
ched	foth	naf	nish
chem	fosh	naj	nib
cham	fash	nij	neb
chom	fush	noj	nub
chim	fesh	nej	nab

MATERIALS
Teacher's Manual, pages 9–10
Assessment Checklist, page 70
token cards
letter cards, including all vowels, consonants, and consonant digraphs *ch, sh, th, wh*

▶ PHONICS

Connecting Sounds to Letters
Spread out the letter cards on the table, making them accessible to a small group of students. Place three different tokens in a row on the table.

- Say it slowly: **Meb.** Point to the first token and say: **What sound does this make?** When the student says /m/, ask: **Can you find the letter that makes that sound?** Have the student place the letter *m* below the first token.

- Say it slowly: **Meb.** Point to the middle token and say: **What sound does this make?** When the student says /e/, ask: **Can you find the letter that makes that sound?** Have the student place the letter *e* below the second token.

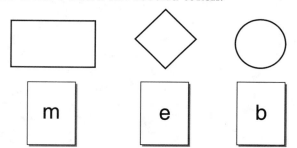

- Say it slowly: **Meb.** Point to the last token and say: **What sound does this make?** When the student says /b/, ask: **Can you find the letter that makes that sound?** Have the student place the letter *b* below the last token.

▶ SUBSTITUTION ROUTINES

Initial Consonants
Remove the three tokens, working with the letter cards only. Say: **If this says** *meb*, **watch as I find the letter that will make the nonsense word** *feb.* Replace the *m* with the *f.* **Now it's your turn. Can you make** *cheb?* As the student replaces the *f* with the card that says *ch*, you may want to review consonant digraphs. Explain that although *ch, sh, th,* and *wh* have two letters, each pair of letters represents one sound.

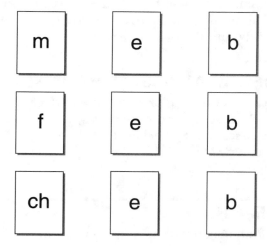

Final Consonants
Invite the next student to find letter cards to make the nonsense word *chez*, then substitute the final letters to make *ched* and *chem.*

Medial Vowels
- Have another student work with changing the medial letter in *chem*, by substituting the short vowel, as in *cham, chom,* and *chim.*

- As you continue having students manipulate letter cards in the initial, medial, and final positions, you may wish to refer to page 72 for additional three-sound nonsense words.

▶ READING ROUTINES

Blending Sounds

- Place the nonsense word *rop* in front of students. Ask the first student: **Can you read the word?** If the student can read the word, ask the next student to read another word.

- If students are having difficulty reading any of the nonsense words, point to each letter and ask them to say the sound. If they are able to segment each sound but are having difficulty blending the sounds together to form the word, take apart the word. Cover up the *r* in *rop*. Ask students to blend *op*, conducting them as they say the sounds.

- Remind them not to stop in between each sound, keeping the two sounds continuous. When they can say the two sounds together quickly, uncover the *r* and ask them to read the nonsense word, blending the sounds together slowly, then more quickly, and finally as one word.

▶ INFORMAL ASSESSMENT

To assess whether students are able to decode three-sound, short-vowel nonsense words, you may want to use the Assessment Checklist found on page 70 in the Teacher's Manual. Use the sample checklist on this page as a guideline.

Teacher Tip

If . . . students aren't able to get eight out of ten nonsense words correct,
Then . . . determine whether they are having difficulty hearing sounds in the initial, final, or medial position. You may want to review particular consonant or vowel sounds in Chapter 1, or do more sound-stretching activities that focus on a particular position.

ASSESSMENT CHECKLIST

Place letter cards on the table. Say each word slowly. Have students take turns saying and spelling each word. Record student performance here for your records.

	Student name	Nonsense or real word	Score	Notes
1.	Maria	fam	+	
2.	Todd	gis	-	gos
3.	Sam	mosh	+	
4.	Maria	cuj	+	
5.	Todd	luf	+	
6.	Sam	rop	+	
7.	Maria	wak	+	
8.	Todd	chev	+	
9.	Sam	gim	+	
10.	Maria	daz	-	das
11.	Todd	juz	+	
12.	Sam	lesh	+	
13.	Maria	bim	+	
14.	Todd	thut	+	
15.	Sam	min	+	
16.	Maria	leth	+	
17.	Todd	zath	+	
18.	Sam	tib	+	
19.	Maria	kem	-	cem
20.	Todd	whit	-	whid
21.	Sam	naz	+	
22.	Maria	shib	+	
23.	Todd	feb	+	
24.	Sam	vel	+	
25.	Maria	thap	+	
26.	Todd	wham	+	
27.	Sam	roch	-	rosh
28.	Maria	meb	+	
29.	Todd	bam	-	pam
30.	Sam	pid	+	

Score:
Maria   8 out of 10
Todd   7 out of 10
Sam   9 out of 10

Sample Assessment Checklist

Teacher Tip

If . . . you've placed a word in front of a student who cannot read it aloud,
Then . . . have the student sound out each letter, then blend. If the attempt is not accurate, the student goes to the vowel as the nucleus of the syllable and identifies it. Then the student adds one consonant before or after the vowel (whichever is easier to say) and blends them. The student says that piece whole, adds one more consonant, then blends together. The student adds additional consonants one by one until the entire word is constructed.

LESSON 1

OBJECTIVES

- Students will recognize that double consonants such as *ff*, *ll*, and *ss* stand for only one sound
- Students will recognize that words with *ck* stand for only one sound
- Students will identify short-vowel words containing double consonants and words with *ck*

WORD BANK OF REAL WORDS

ff	ll	ss	ck
puff	will	pass	back
cuff	full	boss	pick
tiff	hill	less	kick
stuff	fell	miss	duck
buff	well	mess	pack

MATERIALS

Teacher's Manual, page 11
Worktext, page 10

▶ SPELLING

Double Consonants and Words With *ck*

- Write the following categories on chart paper or the board: **ff**, **ll**, **ss**, and **ck**. Explain to students that when they see words spelled with two consonants next to each other, it signals that the vowel before it is short. Write the following words under each category: **puff**, **will**, **pass**, and **back**. Say each word slowly, emphasizing the final consonant sound.

- Point out that even though *ck* is spelled with two letters, it stands for only one sound, /k/.

- Mention that many double consonants stand for only one sound. Have them brainstorm other words that end with these double consonants and write them under the correct categories.

- Have students turn to page 10 in their Worktexts. You may wish to have students work in pairs to complete the spelling activities.

SPELLING RULE
When you see a word spelled with two consonants next to each other after a vowel, that vowel will be short, as in *miss*. The two consonants stand for only one sound, as in *fill* or *kick*.

A. Say the Words
Say each word in the Word Bank. Remember that the two consonants stand for only one sound.

WORD BANK				
hill	boss	pick	kick	puff
fell	buff	miss	duck	mess
back	full	stuff	will	less
pass	pack	cliff	well	cuff

B. Sort the Words
Look at the spelling of each word in the Word Bank. Sort and write each word under the correct category. Circle the two consonants.

ll	ss	ff	ck
_____	_____	_____	_____
_____	_____	_____	_____
_____	_____	_____	_____
_____	_____	_____	_____

C. Fill in the Blanks
Add two consonants at the end of the following letters to make real words. Some of these words may not be found in the Word Bank.

1. bo __ __   3. bla __ __   5. le __ __   7. sha __ __   9. cu __ __
2. chi __ __   4. mo __ __   6. fe __ __   8. pa __ __   10. hi __ __

D. Find the Words
Use a dictionary to find four other words that end with a double consonant or *ck*. Write them below.

_____   _____

Worktext page 10

Teacher Tip

If . . . students cannot tell what sounds are in a word to encode it,
Then . . .

1. Teach them to say the word slowly with you a couple of times, then mouth the word and direct them in saying it. Next, they say it alone. They can hear sounds in words if the word is said more slowly, but not if it is said at the normal rate of speech.

2. If they still can't hear individual sounds when a word is said slowly, warn them and then point to their mouth when they are saying it slowly. This helps them focus attention on what their mouth is doing at the moment they are saying a particular sound.

3. If they still can't hear the sound, have them say the word slowly. When you point, they "freeze" their mouth and stop their voice box. When you point again, they start their voice box again with their mouth "frozen" in place. Then stop again, start again. The effect is that they have segmented the sound.

LESSON 2

OBJECTIVES

- Students will decode and read three-phoneme, short-vowel words
- Students will build and spell short-vowel words using letter cards
- Students will practice reading short-vowel words by unscrambling sounds, finding them on a Word-Search Board, and playing a vowel substitution game

WORD BANK OF REAL WORDS

chat	man	pet	tan	pat
gem	will	pot	much	back
sit	bag	duck	sad	cuff
tug	fog	chin	met	pick
nap	shop	lip	job	tub

MATERIALS

Worktext, pages 11–13
Teacher's Manual, pages 12–14
Assessment Checklist, page 70
Award Certificate, page 71
letter cards for each pair of students

▶ SUBSTITUTION ROUTINES

Initial, Final, and Medial Letters

- On chart paper or the board, write the word **chat**. Ask students to read the word, then write it down on paper. Below *chat*, ask them to write the word *bat*. Ask them to think of other words that rhyme with *chat* and *bat*, and write them underneath. Remind them that the phonogram *at* will remain the same, while they will substitute the initial consonant. Afterward, ask students to share their words.

- On the board, write **man**, and have students read and write it on their papers. Now ask them to substitute the final consonant to build new words, such as *mat* and *map*.

- Have students read and write **pat**, then substitute the short vowel with other vowels to build *pet*, *pit*, *pot*, and *put*.

▶ SHIFTING ROUTINES

Place the letter cards in front of students. Say: **If this says *tap*, how would you spell *pat*?** Invite a volunteer to manipulate the two consonants to spell the new word. Explain that you shifted the initial and final

letter cards to make another word. Repeat this routine, asking students to write down their responses, with words such as *ten* (*net*), *not* (*ton*), *pit* (*tip*), *gum* (*mug*), *nap* (*pan*), and so on.

▶ WORD-BUILDING ROUTINES

- Words with short *a*: Provide each pair of students with a set of letter cards. Ask them to pull the following letters from the pile: *a, t, n, p, c, f, m, r*. Have them build and write down as many short *a* words as they can in five minutes. Remind students that the initial sound in their word will be a consonant; the second a vowel; and the final a consonant, such as in the word *p-a-t*.

- Award a point to the pair with the most words written and read correctly. Continue the game, having students build other short-vowel words using the letter cards listed below.

- Words with short *e*: *e, b, p, m, l, g, d, n, t*
- Words with short *i*: *i, n, t, g, b, f, p, w*
- Words with short *o*: *o, t, n, p, h, s, d, c*
- Words with short *u*: *u, g, n, p, t, b, c, r*

As students continue the word-building game, award points to each student or pair of students who write and read their new words correctly. Award a certificate found on page 71 to the winning team.

Teacher Tip

As your students work through each chapter and become more proficient in their reading and spelling skills, you may want to post their award certificates on a bulletin board. At the completion of *Getting Ready*, honor the award winners with a special ceremony, reflecting on everyone's efforts as they achieve their personal best. For students who continue to struggle but persevere to make the effort, award them with the certificate found on page 71 to commend their efforts.

► PRACTICE

A. Unscramble the Words

Have students work on page 11 in the Worktext to unscramble three-sound, short-vowel words. Review the concept that each word requires a vowel sound in the medial or middle position.

B. Word-Search Board

On Worktext page 12, have students take turns reading the words found in the Word Bank. Then have them work independently to find all 24 words that are hidden.

C. Word Race

Have students work in pairs to play the game found on Worktext page 13. Before playing, read the directions aloud to the class and provide examples of how to change the vowel sound in a word, such as *tip* to *top* to *tap*.

► INFORMAL ASSESSMENT

To assess whether students are able to decode three-sound, short-vowel words, you can use the Assessment Checklist found on page 70 in this manual, or write the Word Bank words on flash cards to test students.

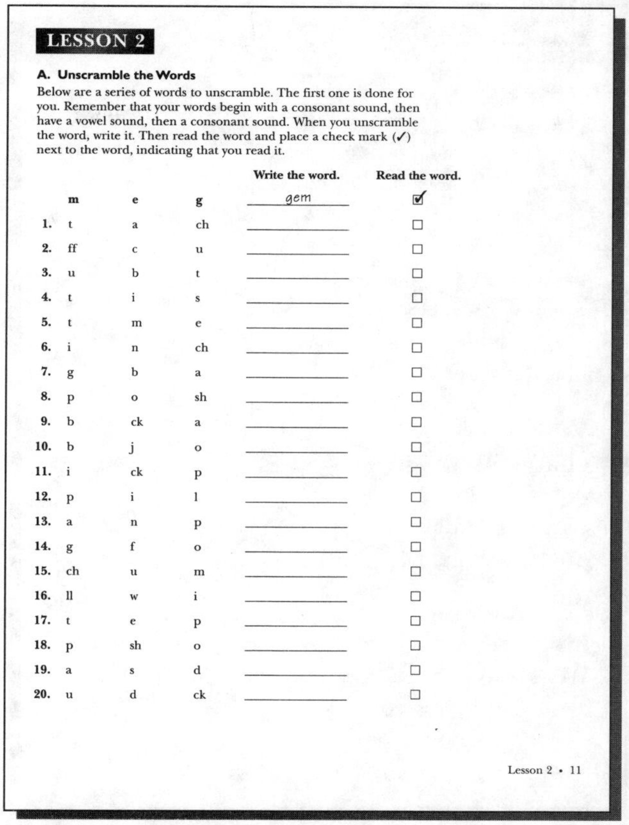

LESSON 2

A. Unscramble the Words

Below are a series of words to unscramble. The first one is done for you. Remember that your words begin with a consonant sound, then have a vowel sound, then a consonant sound. When you unscramble the word, write it. Then read the word and place a check mark (✓) next to the word, indicating that you read it.

				Write the word.	Read the word.
	m	e	g	*gem*	☑
1.	t	a	ch	_____	☐
2.	ff	c	u	_____	☐
3.	u	b	t	_____	☐
4.	t	i	s	_____	☐
5.	t	m	e	_____	☐
6.	i	n	ch	_____	☐
7.	g	b	a	_____	☐
8.	p	o	sh	_____	☐
9.	b	ck	a	_____	☐
10.	b	j	o	_____	☐
11.	i	ck	p	_____	☐
12.	p	i	l	_____	☐
13.	a	n	p	_____	☐
14.	g	f	o	_____	☐
15.	ch	u	m	_____	☐
16.	ll	w	i	_____	☐
17.	t	e	p	_____	☐
18.	p	sh	o	_____	☐
19.	a	s	d	_____	☐
20.	u	d	ck	_____	☐

Lesson 2 • 11

Worktext page 11

On the Word-Search Board below, there are 24 hidden words. As you find each word, circle it. The words can go down, across, diagonally, or backward. Then cross the word out in the Word Bank below.

W	L	L	I	H	C	K	T
T	H	T	Y	H	C	C	E
H	M	A	P	U	H	U	N
E	E	C	T	O	D	D	M
N	S	K	P	X	I	E	K
I	S	S	I	M	S	C	C
H	W	H	E	N	H	K	I
C	I	I	E	Q	Z	S	
J	S	G	L	P	U	F	F
S	H	F	I	L	L	W	V

WORD BANK

map	mess	miss	tuck	chill
deck	ten	chop	when	duck
ship	what	dot	dish	tack
chin	pen	will	fill	then
much	sick	puff	wish	

Worktext page 12

C. Word Race

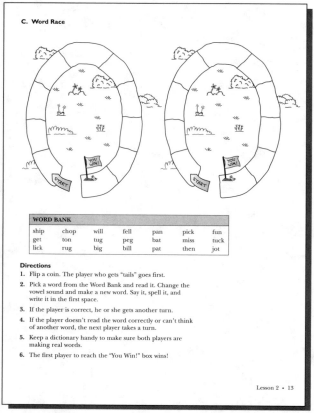

WORD BANK

ship	chop	will	fell	pan	pick	fun
get	ton	tug	peg	bat	miss	tuck
lick	rug	big	bill	pat	then	jot

Directions

1. Flip a coin. The player who gets "tails" goes first.

2. Pick a word from the Word Bank and read it. Change the vowel sound and make a new word. Say it, spell it, and write it in the first space.

3. If the player is correct, he or she gets another turn.

4. If the player doesn't read the word correctly or can't think of another word, the next player takes a turn.

5. Keep a dictionary handy to make sure both players are making real words.

6. The first player to reach the "You Win!" box wins!

Worktext page 13

LESSON 3

OBJECTIVES

- Students will apply their decoding skills by reading tongue-twister sentences that contain three-sound, short-vowel words
- Students will sort words according to their vowel sounds
- Students will decode and read a poem
- Students will write sentences that sequence the order of events in the poem

MATERIALS

Worktext, pages 14–17
Teacher's Manual, pages 15–16
Award Certificate, page 71

▶ DECODING AND READING

A. Wacky Tongue Twisters

- Read aloud the directions found on Worktext page 14. Guide students in reading each of the tongue twisters. Almost all of the words have a three-sound, short-vowel pattern. Point out any words that don't follow this pattern, such as *pickles*. When students come to this word, have them cover up *les* and decode the word *pick*. Guide them in blending both syllables together.

- When students have practiced the tongue twisters and can read them smoothly, have them use a stop watch or the second hand on the classroom clock to see how many times they can read each tongue twister in a minute.

Award a certificate to the student who not only read it the most times, but read it correctly.

B. Sort for Short-Vowel Words

Have students read "Pal and the Pickle Pot" again. Help them begin the sorting activity by asking students to find the first short-vowel word in the tongue twister. Ask them to write it beneath the correct category. Then have students complete the activity independently.

C. Make Up Your Own Tongue Twister

Have students make up their own tongue twisters to share with classmates.

D. My Dog, Red

Have students read the poem silently. Afterward, ask them to circle any words they had difficulty sounding out. Invite students to take turns reading the poem aloud. Coach them in decoding words that are giving them difficulty.

E. What Happens First, Next, and Last?

Have students reread the poem. Taking turns, have them describe the sequence of events in their own words. On Worktext page 17, ask them to write four sentences for each stanza, ordering the events in the proper sequence.

▶ ASSESSMENT

Dictation Routine

Have students write down each sentence as you dictate it. Say the sentence a few times before having them write it. When you're ready for them to write, say each word slowly. If students are having a problem with a particular word, have them write as much of the word as they can.

1. Pat and Peg put the pet pig in a pig pen.
2. Todd will tap on the top of a tin can.
3. Sam and Sal sell shells in a shop.
4. Meg and Mack mop up the mud.
5. Biff has a bug box on his big bed.
6. We go to the vet when my pet is sick.
7. I will put the mop in my van.
8. Red will sit in my lap, and I will pet him.

LESSON 3

A. Wacky Tongue Twisters

On this page, you will read five tongue twisters. Practice reading them with a partner, sounding out any words that you don't know. When you are able to read them smoothly, see how many times you can read one tongue twister in a minute. Remember, you have to read each word correctly. If you don't, please start over. Good luck!

> **Pal and the Pickle Pot**
>
> Pat, Pam, and Peg put Pal, the pet pig, and the pot of pickles in a pig pen. Pal and his pig friends Pit, Pug, and Pod pigged out on the pickle pot!

> **Tuck and the Thin, Tan, Tin Can**
>
> Tom and Tim tell Todd to tug with Tuck, the pup. Then Todd and Tuck go tap, tap, tap on the top of that thin, tan, tin can.

> **Sam and His Sis Sal**
>
> Sam and his sis Sal sit in the sun and eat a sub as they sell a sack of six shells by a shop. "Such fun," said Sam and his sis Sal.

> **My Mutt Mack**
>
> Matt, Meg, and Mom mop up the mud mess that my mutt Mack made. How much mud did Meg, Mom, and Matt mop up?

> **Biff's Big Bed**
>
> Ben, Bob, and Biff put a bell, bag, bat, and bug box on top of Biff's big bed.

Worktext page 14

B. Sort for Short-Vowel Words

Read **Pal and the Pickle Pot** again. Then look for words that have a short-vowel sound and sort them according to each sound.

Title: _Pal and the Pickle Pot_

short a	short e	short i	short o	short u
_____	_____	_____	_____	_____
_____	_____	_____	_____	_____
_____	_____	_____	_____	_____

Choose another tongue twister. Write its title below. Sort the short-vowel words according to each sound.

Title: _____

short a	short e	short i	short o	short u
_____	_____	_____	_____	_____
_____	_____	_____	_____	_____
_____	_____	_____	_____	_____

C. Make Up Your Own Tongue Twister

Choose a consonant, such as *p, t, s, m,* or *b.* Using a dictionary, look up words that begin with that letter and have a short-vowel sound. Create your own tongue twister and write it below. Invite your friends to practice reading it. See how many times each friend can read it correctly in one minute.

Title: _____

_____

_____

_____

_____

Worktext page 15

D. My Dog, Red

Read this poem to yourself. Then practice reading it aloud with a partner, sounding out any words that you don't know.

> **My Dog, Red**
>
> I will wash my dog, Red.
> And when he is fed
> I will pet him and then
> We will sit on my bed.
>
> And when Red is sick
> We will go to the vet.
> Red will lick the man's chin
> And get him all wet!
>
> Then Red and I
> Will go to the shop
> To get a big pot,
> A pan, and a mop.
>
> I will put the big pot,
> The mop, and the pan
> And my pet dog, Red,
> In my big, big tan van.
>
> And when we get home
> Red will sit in my lap.
> I will pet him and then
> We will take a big nap!

Worktext page 16

E. What Happens First, Next, and Last?

Read the poem "My Dog, Red" again. Notice that in each stanza, the teenager did something with her dog, Red. First, tell a classmate all the things they did together. For each of the five stanzas, write four sentences about what they did. Be sure to put the sentences in the correct sequence.

1. _____

_____

_____

2. _____

_____

_____

3. _____

_____

_____

4. _____

_____

_____

5. _____

_____

_____

Worktext page 17

CHAPTER 3
Other Three-Sound Words

TOKEN LESSON A

OBJECTIVES

- Students will develop phonemic awareness by segmenting nonsense words comprised of three sounds, using tokens to represent these sounds
- Students will discriminate sounds in the initial, final, and medial positions
- Students will discriminate sounds through the deletions of initial and final consonants

WORD BANK OF NONSENSE WORDS

seev	moez	dawm	naish	soob
loik	gaish	deeg	towp	mooth
laip	laish	muesh	shoob	seef
rawg	vaud	vead	zaid	noat

WORD BANK OF REAL WORDS

pail	boat	nail	reef	fail
seem	need	dawn	coin	goat
weed	sail	coat	rail	leaf
fawn	lawn	shoot	yawn	beet

MATERIALS

Teacher's Manual, pages 17–18
token cards
additional list of nonsense words, page 72

Teacher Tip

Before beginning this chapter, you may want to review long-vowel sounds, diphthongs, and vowel pairs, found in Chapter 1, pages 4–6.

▶ PHONEMIC AWARENESS

Segmenting Sounds

Place three different tokens in a row, such as a diamond, square, and circle.

- Say it slowly: *Seev.* **What is the first sound you hear in *seev*?** As you say the word, stretch and elongate each sound, without segmenting it. As the first student says /s/, have him or her point to the diamond, which represents the initial consonant sound.

- Say it slowly: *Seev.* **What is the next sound you hear in *seev*?** Have the student begin saying the nonsense word, and cut him or her off after saying /ee/. When the student identifies /ee/, have him or her point to the square or token representing the medial vowel sound.

- Say it slowly: *Seev.* **What is the final sound you hear in *seev*?** After the student says /v/, have him or her touch the circle representing the final consonant sound.

- Invite another student to segment a new word, using nonsense words found in the Word Bank.

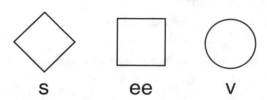

▶ SUBSTITUTION ROUTINES

Initial Consonants

Place three new tokens in front of students, such as a star, rectangle, and triangle.

- Say: **This says *loik*. Now I'm going to make *boik*.** Replace the star with a circle.

- Say: **If this now says *boik*, I'm going to make *noik*.** Replace the circle with a square.

- Say: **If this now says *noik*, I'm going to make *zoik*.** Replace the square with a diamond.

- After modeling this routine, pick another word from the Word Bank of Nonsense Words and rotate students, having each substitute the initial consonant sounds, such as *laip*, *maip*, *vaip*, *daip*.

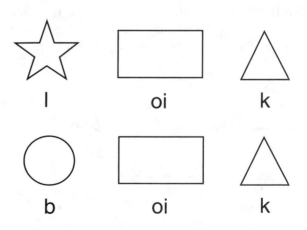

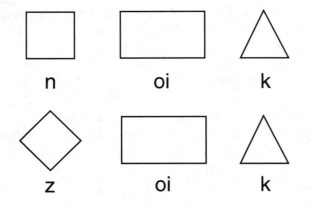

Final Consonants

Place three new tokens in front of students, such as a square, circle, and diamond.

- Say: **If this says *shoob*, make *shoov*.** Have the student replace the diamond with another token, such as a star. Guide students in substituting the final consonant sounds, replacing the last token with a new one.

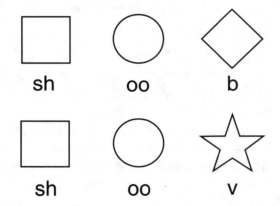

Medial Vowel Sounds

Place a triangle, circle, and star on the table.

- Say: **If this says *vaud*, make *vood*.** Coach students in substituting the medial vowel sound to make other nonsense words, such as *veed*, *vued*, and *voad*.

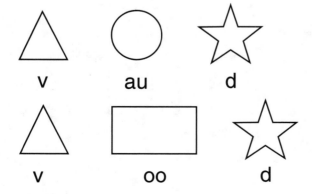

▶ **DELETION ROUTINES**

Initial and Final Consonants

Place a circle, rectangle, and square on the table.

- Say: **If this says *dawm*, make *awm*.** Coach students in taking away the circle token, which represents the initial consonant sound. Once students become proficient at this, replace the circle and have them delete the final consonant sound to make *daw*, taking away the square.
- Repeat this deletion routine with other nonsense words.

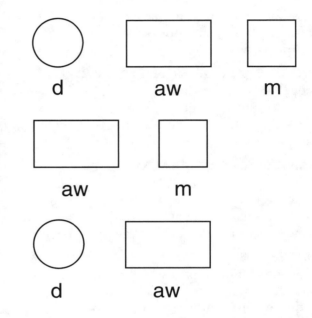

- For additional three-sound, long-vowel nonsense words, turn to page 72.
- After students have worked with three-sound, long-vowel nonsense words, you can use the Word Bank of Real Words with them.

TOKEN LESSON B

OBJECTIVES

- Students will segment three-sound nonsense words comprised of long vowels and vowel pairs by connecting sounds to letters
- Students will make and read new nonsense words by substituting beginning, final, and medial sounds and letters

WORD BANK OF NONSENSE WORDS

List 1	List 2	List 3	List 4
voon	seeg	moish	foat
choon	sheeg	thoish	zoat
thoon	heeg	roish	loat
thooz	heem	roich	loash
thood	heech	roith	loaz
thoom	heef	roid	loag
thaum	hoaf	raed	leeg
thiem	hauf	ruud	laug
theem	hoif	rowd	loog

MATERIALS

Teacher's Manual, pages 19–20
Assessment Checklist, page 70
token cards
letter cards, including all vowels, vowel pairs, consonants, and consonant digraphs

▶ PHONICS

Connecting Sounds to Letters

Make a set of letter cards accessible to a small group of students. Place three different-shaped tokens in front of them.

- Say it slowly: **Voon.** Point to the first token and say: **What sound does this make?** When the student says /v/, ask: **Can you find the letter that makes that sound?** Have the student place the letter *v* below the first token.
- Say it slowly: **Voon.** Point to the middle token and say: **What sound does this make?** When the student says /oo/, ask: **Can you find the vowel pair that makes that sound?** Have the student place the letters *oo* below the second token.
- Say it slowly: **Voon.** Point to the last token and say: **What sound does this make?** When the student says /n/, ask: **Can you find the letter that makes that sound?** Ask the student to place the letter *n* below the third token.
- Repeat this routine with other students in the group, using nonsense words from the Word Bank.

▶ SUBSTITUTION ROUTINES

Initial Consonants

Once students are able to identify and connect the sounds to letters, remove the tokens, working with letter cards only.

- Say: **If this says *seeg*, watch as I find the letter card that will make the nonsense word *sheeg*.** Replace the *s* with the consonant digraph *sh*.
- Say: **Now it's your turn. Can you make *heeg*?** Coach the student in locating the letter card *h*.
- Repeat this routine until students are proficient at substituting letter cards in the initial position.

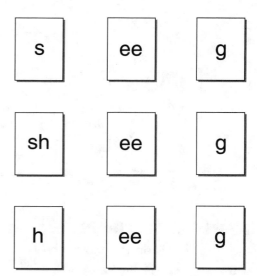

Final Consonants

Invite another student to find letter cards to make new nonsense words, substituting final consonants, such as *heem*, *heech*, and *heef*.

Medial Vowels

- Have the next student manipulate the letter cards in the medial position by substituting vowel sounds, such as *hoaf*, *hauf*, and *hoif*.
- For additional nonsense words, refer to page 72.

▶ DELETION ROUTINES

Initial and Final Consonants

Place the following letter cards in front of students: *f-oa-t*.

- Say: **If this says *foat*, make *oat*.** Ask a student to remove the first letter card.

- Say: **If this says *foat*, make *foa*.** Have the student remove the last letter card.

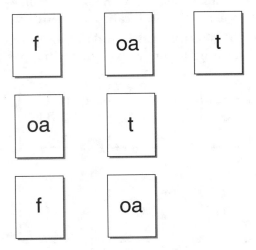

▶ SHIFTING ROUTINES

Place these letter cards on the table: *m-ee-th*.

- Say: **If this says *meeth*, make *theem*.** Coach students in shifting the initial and final letter cards.

- Say: **If this says *theem*, make *eemth*.** If students are having trouble with shifting letter card positions, stretch out each sound, saying the word very slowly. Also let them know that no letter cards, other than the three in front of them are needed.

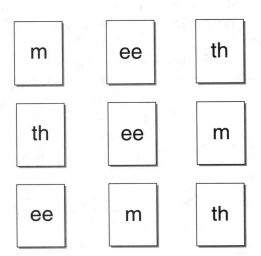

▶ READING ROUTINES

Blending Sounds

- Place the word *loag*—as a whole word—in front of students. Ask one student to read the word. If the student reads it correctly, move on to the next student and have him or her decode another nonsense word.

- When students have difficulty reading a particular word, point to each letter and ask them to say the sound. If they are able to segment each sound, but if they are having difficulty blending the sounds together to form the word, you may want to take apart the word. Cover up the *l* in *loag*. Coach students in sounding out *oag*, conducting them to say the sound in a continuous fashion. Then ask students to blend the *oa-g* more quickly. Now uncover the *l*, getting them to read the nonsense word, blending the sounds together slowly, then more quickly, and finally as one word.

▶ INFORMAL ASSESSMENT

Use the Assessment Checklist on page 70 to determine whether students are able to decode three-sound, long-vowel, and vowel-pair patterns.

Teacher Tip

If... students aren't able to get eight out of ten nonsense words correct,

Then... assess whether they are having difficulty hearing sounds in the initial, final, or medial positions. You may want to review particular consonants, long vowels, or vowel pairs in Chapter 1.

LESSON 1 (Part 1)

OBJECTIVES

- Students will recognize that when a word with one syllable has two vowels, the first vowel usually has a long sound, while the second vowel is silent

- Students will identify vowel-consonant-*e* spelling patterns

- Students will look at word pairs to distinguish short- and long-vowel patterns, such as *slid/slide*

WORD BANK OF REAL WORDS

mad/made	hid/hide	rob/robe
cub/cube	can/cane	rid/ride
hop/hope	tub/tube	pan/pane
kit/kite	cur/cure	dud/dude
tap/tape	dim/dime	mop/mope
cut/cute	fat/fate	bit/bite
not/note	cop/cope	

MATERIALS

Worktext, page 18
Teacher's Manual, page 21

CHAPTER 3 LESSON 1 (Part 1)

SPELLING RULE
Long-vowel words can be spelled vowel-consonant-e, as in *make, time, hope,* and *cute.* When a word with one syllable has two vowels, the first vowel will say its name, while the e is silent.

A. Say the Words
Say each word in the Word Bank. Remember that the first vowel will say its name, while the *e* will be silent.

WORD BANK

note	fate	pane	bite	tape
cube	dime	mope	robe	dude
hide	cane	ride	cope	cute
kite	cure	tube	hope	made

B. Sort the Words
Look at the spelling of each word in the Word Bank. Sort and write each word under the correct long-vowel category. Circle the vowel that says its name.

a-consonant-e	i-consonant-e	o-consonant-e	u-consonant-e
_____	_____	_____	_____
_____	_____	_____	_____
_____	_____	_____	_____
_____	_____	_____	_____
_____	_____	_____	_____

C. Fill in the Blanks
Add a vowel and then a silent *e* to make real words. These are words that are found in the Word Bank.

1. c__t__   3. t__p__   5. b__t__   7. d__m__   9. f__t__
2. m__p__   4. n__t__   6. d__d__   8. k__t__   10. r__d__

D. Make It Short
Each word in the Word Bank can be turned into a short-vowel word by dropping the *e*, as in *made* to *mad.* Read each word, then think of the short-vowel word. Write four word pairs, such as *made/mad* below:

_____   _____   _____   _____

18 • Chapter 3

Worktext page 18

▶ **SPELLING**

Vowel-consonant-e patterns

- Write the following categories on the board: *a*-consonant-*e*, *i*-consonant-*e*, *o*-consonant-*e*, and *u*-consonant-*e*. Explain to students that some long-vowel words can be spelled vowel-consonant-*e*, as in *make, time, hope,* and *cute*. As you say each word, write it under the correct categories. Mention that when a word with one syllable has two vowels, the first vowel will say its name, while the *e* is silent. To help them remember the rule, you can say: **When two vowels go a-walking, the first one does the talking!**

- Have students turn to page 18 in their Worktexts and complete the activities. Coach students who are having difficulty in reading or sorting their words.

- After students complete the "Make It Short" activity, ask them to read their short-vowel and long-vowel word pairs to make sure they are pronouncing the vowel sounds correctly.

LESSON 1 (Part 2)

OBJECTIVES

- Students will recognize that when two vowels are next to each other in a one-syllable word, the first one says its name, while the second one is silent
- Students will identify long-vowel words with *ee*, *ea*, *ai*, *ay*, and *oa*
- Students will recognize that homophones are words that sound alike but have different spelling patterns

WORD BANK OF REAL WORDS

beet	beat	paid	pay	coat
meet	meat	maid	may	boat
cheep	cheap	nail	say	foam
feet	feat	gain	day	goal
peek	peak	fail	hay	soap

MATERIALS

Worktext, page 19
Teacher's Manual, page 22

LESSON 1 (Part 2)

SPELLING RULE
When two vowels are together in a word, the first one usually says its name, while the second one is silent, such as in *meat* or *coat*.

WORD BANK

soap	way	nail	coat	hay	boat
peak	gain	day	feet	paid	beat
beet	meat	maid	cheep	meet	goal
cheap	may	peek	foam	feat	pay

A. Say the Words
Say each word in the Word Bank. Remember that the first vowel will say its name, while the second vowel is silent.

B. Sort the Words
Look at the spelling of each word in the Word Bank. Sort and write each word under the correct long-vowel category. Circle the vowel that says its name.

ee	ea	ai	ay	oa

C. Fill in the Blanks
Add two vowels to make each word. All of the words are found in the Word Bank. There is more than one possible answer for some of these words.

1. m __ __ t
2. f __ __ m
3. f __ __ t
4. p __ __ k
5. d __ y
6. c __ __ t
7. b __ __ t
8. n __ __ l

D. Homophones
Homophones are words that sound alike, but are spelled differently and have different meanings, such as *beat* and *beet*. Write four other word pairs that are homophones below.

1. _____ and _____
2. _____ and _____
3. _____ and _____
4. _____ and _____

Lesson 1 • 19

Worktext page 19

▶ SPELLING

Long Vowels

- Write the following categories on the board: **ee**, **ea**, **ai**, **ay**, **oa**. Explain to students that when a word with one syllable has two vowels, the first vowel usually has a long sound, while the second vowel is silent. Write words from the Word Bank as you explain each long-vowel sound.

- Ask students to complete Worktext page 19. Help students decode each word, then help them to sort them according to their sounds and spellings. Point out that each word in the "Fill in the Blanks" activity can be found in their Word Bank.

- Explain to students that homophones are words that sound alike but are spelled differently and don't have the same meaning, such as *beat* and *beet*. Say the following sentences to point out the differences: **We're a team that can't be beat. I'll slice a beet and put it in my salad.** Have them look in their Word Bank to find four other homophone word pairs.

LESSON 2

OBJECTIVES
- Students will decode and read three-phoneme words that contain long-vowel spelling patterns and diphthongs
- Students will build and spell words using letter cards
- Students will practice reading by unscrambling sounds to make words, playing Bingo, and sorting words according to spelling patterns

WORD BANK OF REAL WORDS

read	paid	coin	day	oath
name	moan	say	peak	join
hope	sheep	team	raid	pay
soil	wheel	seem	dime	cheek
tube	boil	heal	may	coal

MATERIALS
Worktext, pages 20–22
Teacher's Manual, pages 23–24
Assessment Checklist, page 70
Award Certificate, page 71
letter cards for each pair of students
tokens for Bingo game

▶ SUBSTITUTION ROUTINES

Initial Sounds

- Write the word **name** on the board. Ask a student to read the word, then have the group members write it down on their papers. Below *name*, ask volunteers to think of words that rhyme with it, such as *game* and *tame*, and have them suggest the spelling for each word and write it underneath *name*. Remind them that the initial consonant needs to be replaced with a new sound each time.

- Repeat this routine with other words in the Word Bank, such as *peak*, *heal*, and *may*. As you do this activity as a whole group, students may encounter rhyming words that are spelled differently, such as *peek*, *beak*, *week*, *seek*, and *leak*. Remind them that although these are all long-vowel words, they are spelled differently.

▶ SORTING ROUTINES

Write each word from the Word Bank on index cards. Have students take turns sorting each word according to the vowel pattern. As students sort, have them read each word aloud.

▶ WORD-BUILDING ROUTINES

- Provide each student or pair of students with a set of letter cards. Determine what vowel pattern you'd like students to practice. For example, if they need more practice with long *a*, specifically *a*-consonant-*e*, ask them to pull the *a* and *e* letter cards along with consonants that will make a lot of words, such as *m, k, l, f, w, t, b, c,* and *r*. As one student makes a word, the other can write it down. Then they can switch roles.

- Time individuals or pairs of students. Award a certificate to the person or pair who makes the most words in a five- or ten-minute period. The certificate can be found on page 71.

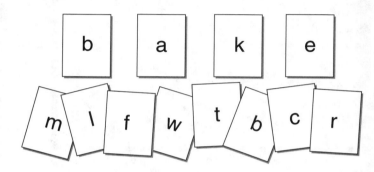

▶ PRACTICE

A. Bingo

Have two or three students play Bingo, using the Bingo cards found on Worktext pages 20–21. Invite one student to be the caller, reading the Word Bank words. Students can use the tokens as chips for each Bingo card.

B. A Word Pattern

- Ask students to turn to page 22 in the Worktext. Tell them that they will be using words from their Word Bank to make a pattern of words in the grid.

- As they write a word in the grid, have them read the word, then cross it out. Award a certificate to the student who was able to use the most words and decode each correctly.

▶ INFORMAL ASSESSMENT

Use the Assessment Checklist found on page 70 to assess whether students can decode and read three-sound words.

LESSON 2

A. Bingo

Directions

1. Each player takes some tokens.
2. Pick a caller.
3. The caller reads a word from the Word Bank in any order.
4. The players put a token on the square that contains the word.
5. The first player to get four tokens in a row says, "Bingo!"

WORD BANK

read	pick	coin	day	oath
name	moan	say	peak	join
hope	sheep	team	raid	pay
soil	wheel	seem	dime	cheek
tube	boil	heal	may	come

Bingo Card 1

dime	heal	soil	seem
read	hope	name	sheep
day	wheel	coin	pay
join	raid	peak	may

Worktext page 20

Bingo Card 2

come	day	read	hope
team	soil	cheek	tube
boil	may	seem	join
moan	oath	say	wheel

Bingo Card 3

pick	name	join	wheel
say	soil	dime	tube
oath	team	raid	boil
heal	may	seem	day

Worktext page 21

B. A Word Pattern

Use words in the Word Bank below to create your own word pattern in the grid. Begin by making another word, using one of the letters in the word *take*. As you use words in the Word Bank, cross them out. The student with the most words in his or her word pattern wins!

WORD BANK

take	seed	ray	mole
cube	coil	meal	seal
rope	deep	mean	shake
white	lead	loan	coin
day	foil	teeth	leak

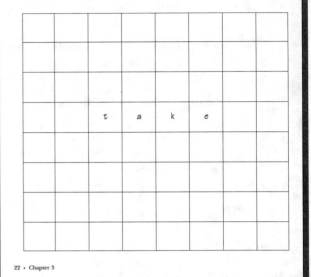

Worktext page 22

LESSON 3

OBJECTIVES

- Students will apply their decoding skills by reading passages containing words with long vowels
- Students will sort words according to their spelling patterns
- Students will read a passage and fill in missing words that contain long-vowel spelling patterns
- Students will write a sports cheer that includes words containing both short and long vowels

MATERIALS

Worktext, pages 23–25
Teacher's Manual, pages 25–26
Award Certificate, page 71

▶ DECODING AND READING

A. Drop Me a Note!

- Coach students as they read letters written by Mike and Kate. As they read, they will be reviewing many short-vowel words. In addition, they will be focusing on reading words containing the long-vowel patterns learned in this chapter.
- Have students practice reading for fluency, then award certificates, found on page 71, to students who are becoming more proficient.

Teacher Tip

Before students read each letter, write any words that may give them difficulty on the board, such as the two-syllable words **over** and **party**. Help them decode these words. Then write **laps** and **miles** on the board. Cover up the *s* in *laps*, have a volunteer read the word, then add /*s*/ to make it plural. Point out the "P.S.," or postscript, in Kate's letter and write the word **join** on the board. Review the sound a diphthong makes in a word. You can refer to page 6 in Chapter 1 of the Teacher's Manual for additional suggestions.

B. Sort for Long-Vowel Words

As a group, reread the letter written by Mike. Then ask students to circle the words with the following long-vowel patterns: *a_e*, *i_e*, *o_e*, *ea*, *ee*, and *oa*. Have them sort the circled words according to their long-vowel spelling pattern.

C. Fill in the Blanks

In this activity, have students read the letter by Kate and fill in the missing long-vowel words using the Word Bank as a guide.

D. A Team Cheer

Before students read the cheer, help them decode the words **three** and **Saturday**, by writing each word on the board.

- Cover up the letters *ree* in *three* and have students say /*th*/. Then cover up the letters *th* and have them sound out /*r*/ and /*ee*/. Ask them to blend the two sounds together. Finally, guide them in blending the three sounds together to make the word.
- Have students look at the word *Saturday* in chunks. Cover up all the letters except *sat* and decode this word first. Then cover up everything except *day* and have them decode that chunk. Next, have them sound out /*ur*/. Finally, blend the whole word together, syllable by syllable.

E. Make Up Your Own Cheer

Take a poll to see which sport the class likes best and have them write a group cheer together.

▶ ASSESSMENT

Dictation Routine

Have students write down each sentence as you dictate it. Say the sentence a few times before having them write. When they're ready, say each sentence slowly and clearly. If students have difficulty figuring out how to spell a particular word, have them leave a blank or write as much of the word as they can.

1. Mike made the team.
2. I need to get in shape.
3. I like to ride my bike and race it.
4. Come to the game this week.
5. Kate will sit with Hope at the game.
6. I will go to the beach with my dog.
7. I need to feed my dog.
8. I may join a team.

A. Drop Me a Note!
Read the two letters below.

> Dear Kate,
>
> I made the team! I need to get in shape by the time I play the game. I will hike up the hill. I will ride my bike and race with Gabe. We will take my boat to the lake. Gabe and I will dive in the lake. Gabe will time me while I do five laps.
>
> Can you come to the game this week? Gabe and Hope will save you a seat. Then we can go on a date when the game is over. I will take you to a party at Nate's house. Gabe will take Hope to the party.
>
> I need to get some sleep. I have to wake up at 6:00 A.M. and ride nine miles on my bike. Drop me a note!
>
> Mike

> Dear Mike,
>
> Way to go! I will go this week to the game. I will cheer for you and the team. I will look for Gabe and Hope and sit with them. Nate's party will be fun too.
>
> I need to take my dog Big Ray for a run at the beach. Then I need to feed him. I can't wait to see you this week. Good luck!
>
> Kate
>
> P.S. I may join a team too!

Lesson 3 • 23

Worktext page 23

B. Sort for Long-Vowel Words
Read the letter by Mike again. Then look for words that have long-vowel sounds and circle them. Sort them according to each sound.

a-consonant-e	i-consonant-e	o-consonant-e
_____	_____	_____
_____	_____	_____
_____	_____	_____
_____	_____	_____
ea	**ee**	**oa**
_____	_____	_____
_____	_____	_____

C. Fill in the Blanks
Read the letter by Kate that is written below. As you read, use your Word Bank to fill in the missing words. Use each word once.

WORD BANK			
team	need	beach	take
feed	game	week	Hope
may	Gabe	wait	

> Dear Mike,
>
> Way to go! I will go this _____ to the _____. I will cheer for you and the _____. I will look for _____ and _____ and sit with them. Nate's party will be fun too.
>
> I _____ to _____ my dog Big Ray for a run at the _____. Then I need to _____ him. I can't _____ to see you this week. Good luck!
>
> Kate
>
> P.S. I _____ join a team too!

24 • Chapter 3

Worktext page 24

D. A Team Cheer
Read the poem below.

> One, three, five, nine.
> See my team. We are so fine!
>
> So join the team. It will be fun.
> We kick the ball. We pass and run.
>
> Each of us is lean and mean.
> We will beat the other team.
>
> We will play this game to win.
> Make the goal and kick it in.
>
> We play ball each Saturday.
> "Win, win, win" is what we say!
>
> We will win. We can't be beat.
> See us play, so take a seat!

E. Make Up Your Own Cheer
Read the cheer again. Think of a sport that you like best. Then make up your own cheer. Use some long-vowel words, such as *team*, *beat*, and *game*. Review some of your short-vowel words, such as *win*, *kick*, and *run*.

Title: _____

_____
_____
_____
_____
_____
_____
_____
_____

Lesson 3 • 25

Worktext page 25

CHAPTER 4
Three-Sound, More Complex Words

TOKEN LESSON A

OBJECTIVES
- Students will develop phonemic awareness by segmenting nonsense words comprised of initial and final consonant blends, using tokens to represent each sound
- Students will discriminate sounds through substitution and deletion routines as well as by shifting the position of sounds

WORD BANK OF NONSENSE WORDS

skai	ploe	tre	fli	smue
gree	dwie	spo	bree	dri
fru	swee	klo	aps	ilf
esk	omp	oest	eebz	inth
ust	ips	ept	aizd	eps

WORD BANK OF REAL WORDS

mask	west	tree	true
must	elf	east	dump
free	greet	ninth	flee
bee	treat	cups	jump

MATERIALS
Teacher's Manual, pages 27–28
token cards
additional list of nonsense words, page 72

▶ PHONEMIC AWARENESS

Segmenting Sounds

Place a circle, rectangle, and triangle in front of a small group of students.

- Say it slowly: *Skai.* **What is the first sound you hear in** *skai*? As you say the word, stretch each sound without segmenting it. Have a student point to the circle and say /s/.

- Say it slowly: *Skai.* **What is the next sound you hear in** *skai*? Have the student stretch out the first two sounds, cutting him or her off after /k/. Ask the student to point to the token representing the second consonant. (*rectangle*)

- Say it slowly: *Skai.* **What is the last sound you hear in** *skai*? Have the student say /ai/, pointing to the triangle at the same time.

- Introduce other nonsense words, rotating them among students in the small group.

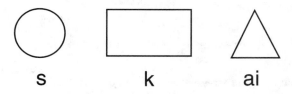

Teacher Tip

Consonant blends can be very difficult for students to hear because they need to distinguish very fine sound differentiations. It is important to model saying each nonsense word very slowly, elongating each sound. As students segment the word, have them listen to and stretch each sound. You can also introduce word pairs, such as *sai/skai, poe/ploe, sue/smue, di/dri*. By working with word pairs, students can compare and hear how a consonant blend sounds different from a single consonant sound.

▶ WORD-PAIR ROUTINES

Making Consonant Blends

Place a star and a diamond next to each other.

- Say: **This says** *ko.* **Now I'm going to make** *klo.* Add a square between the star and diamond. Ask students to say the new sound that was added. (/l/)

- Put a rectangle and circle on the table. Say: **If this says** *fu,* **make** *fru.* As a student places a new token between the rectangle and circle, have him or her say /r/, representing the new consonant.

- Once you've had students work with several initial consonants and consonant blends, use words from the Word Bank of Nonsense Words that have final consonant blends. Say: **If this says** *ek,* **make** *esk.* Students should add a token in the middle of the two sounds and say /s/. Do this routine with other nonsense words, such as *us/ust, eez/eebz,* and *op/omp.*

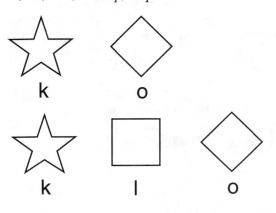

▶ SUBSTITUTION ROUTINES

Initial Consonant Blends

Place a rectangle, circle, and triangle on the table. Substitute consonants to make new consonant blends.

- Say: **If this says** *smue,* **make** *spue.* Ask a volunteer to point to the token that needs to be replaced (*the circle*), while saying the new sound /p/.

- Say: **If this says** *spue,* **make** *skue.* Coach the student in replacing the second token once again to form a new consonant blend.

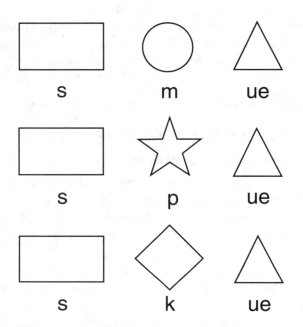

Final Consonant Blends

Use new tokens to have students work with substituting consonants to make final blends, such as *ilf/ ilm/ ilz; omp/ omz/ omd; esk/ esp/ esd.*

▶ SHIFTING ROUTINES

When students are proficient in adding and substituting sounds to make consonant blends, guide them in listening carefully as you shift the position of sounds. This routine can be much more difficult for students to hear, so be sure to stretch each sound as you say it.

- Place a square, triangle, and star on the table. Say: **If this says** *osp,* **make** *pos.* As the student places the star before the square, have him or her segment each sound, /p/ /o/ /s/.

- Say: **If this says** *pos,* **make** *spo.* After the student has placed the triangle, star, and square in a row, have the student point to each token while saying /s/ /p/ /o/.

- Invite students to shift positions of sounds in other nonsense words.

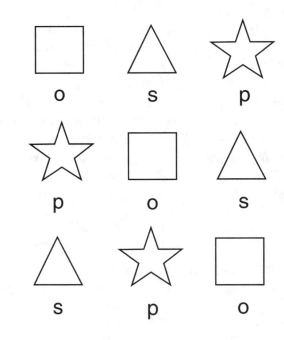

- For additional complex, three-sound nonsense words containing consonant blends, turn to page 72.

- After students have worked with complex, three-sound nonsense words with consonant blends, you can use the Word Bank of Real Words with them.

TOKEN LESSON B

OBJECTIVES

- Students will segment three-sound, more complex words comprised of initial or final consonant blends by connecting sounds to letters
- Students will make and then read new nonsense words by adding, substituting, deleting, or shifting the position of letters

WORD BANK OF NONSENSE WORDS

stoe	bloy	tes	frai	skou
broo	slee	prau	asht	drail
isp	eft	aks	oops	alp
ilk	ort	anth	oemz	uusht

MATERIALS

Teacher's Manual, pages 29–30
Assessment Checklist, page 70
token cards
letter cards, including all vowels, vowel
    pairs, consonants, and consonant digraphs

▶ PHONICS

Connecting Sounds to Letters

Have a set of letter cards handy. Place three different-shaped tokens in front of students.

- Say it slowly: **Stoe.** Point to the first token and say: **What sound does this make?** When the student responds /s/, say: **Find the letter that makes that sound.** Ask the student to place the letter *s* under the first token.

- Say it slowly: **Stoe.** Point to the middle token and say: **What sound does this make?** Have the student place the letter *t* below the second token and say /t/.

- Say it slowly: **Stoe.** Point to the last token and say: **What sound does this make?** When the student says /oe/, ask: **Can you find the letter(s) that make this sound?** The student may place the letter(s) *o* or *oe* beneath the last token.

- Repeat this routine using other nonsense words from the Word Bank. Be sure to practice both initial and final consonant blends.

▶ SUBSTITUTION ROUTINES

Initial Consonant Blends

Once students are proficient in identifying and connecting the sounds to letters, remove the tokens and use letter cards only.

- Say: **If this says *bloy*, make *broy*.** As you say the word slowly, emphasize the second consonant. Guide students in finding the letter *r* and substituting it for the *l*.

- Say: **If this says *broy*, make *skoy*.** Ask students how many sounds have been changed, coaching them to substitute *br* with *sk*.

- Say: **If this says *skoy*, make *sloy*.** Invite a volunteer to substitute /k/ with /l/.

- Repeat this routine with other nonsense words until all students have had multiple opportunities to manipulate initial consonant sounds.

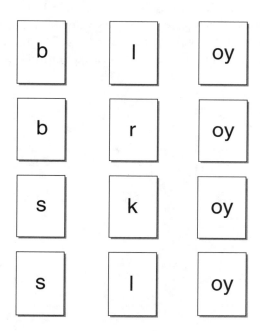

Final Consonant Blends

Mention to students that in this routine, you will be substituting consonants at the end of each nonsense word and that they should listen carefully for those sounds.

- Say: **If this says *anth*, make *anz*.** Help students substitute the *th* letter card with the *z*.

- Say: **If this says *anz*, make *anch*.** Students should substitute the letter *z* with the consonant digraph *ch*.

- Say: **If this says *anch*, make *anf*.** Invite a student to substitute *ch* with the letter *f*.

- Continue this routine with other nonsense words containing final consonant blends.

▶ DELETION ROUTINES

Tell students that you will be deleting a consonant somewhere in each nonsense word and ask them to listen carefully as you stretch out each sound.

- Say: **If this says *frai*, make *rai*.** As students remove the *f*, ask them to say the new word *rai*.

- Repeat this routine with other nonsense words, such as *slee/ see, alp/ ap, uusht/ uush.*

▶ SHIFTING ROUTINES

Mention to students that you are going to challenge them with another routine. Explain that you will be shifting the position of letters within the word, which may be more difficult for them to hear.

- Say: **If this says *slee*, make *seel*.** Repeat each word slowly, stretching out each sound. Once students have shifted the *l* to the end of the word, continue the routine using the same letter cards to make *lees* and *eels*. You may want to demonstrate this routine by providing students with a few examples before they attempt it themselves.

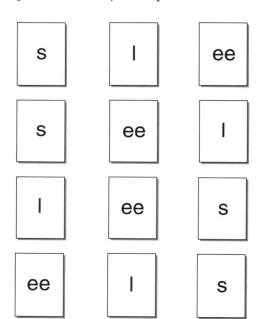

▶ READING ROUTINES
Blending Sounds

After having students practice spelling nonsense words, assess their ability to read the nonsense words that they are making.

- Place the word *prau* in front of students and invite a volunteer to read it. If the student reads it correctly, move on to the next volunteer and place another nonsense word on the table for that student to read.

- If students have difficulty decoding the nonsense words, coach them in stretching out each sound that makes the consonant blend, so that they don't skip over one of these sounds. You can also point out the differences in what a word sounds like with and without the consonant blend, such as in *skou/ sou, oops/ oop,* and *eft/ et.*

▶ INFORMAL ASSESSMENT

Use the Assessment Checklist on page 70 to determine whether students are able to decode and read three-sound nonsense words that contain initial and final consonant blends.

Teacher Tip

If . . . a student says a consonant blend together (e.g., /*pl*/) and assigns one token for the blend,

Then . . . ask: **How many sounds do you hear in /*pl*/? What is the first sound?** When the student identifies it, ask: **What is the second sound?** Then help the student assign two tokens to the blend.

LESSON 1 (Part 1)

OBJECTIVES

- Students will recognize that consonant *c* can sound like /*k*/ or /*s*/
- Students will identify words containing both sounds
- Students will sort words according to their sounds and read sentences to fill in words with hard *c* and soft *c*

WORD BANK OF REAL WORDS

candy	celery	actor	cattle	recess
coal	city	coin	dice	coat
cat	race	cut	rice	cap
cake	mice	cone	face	ice

MATERIALS

Worktext, page 26
Teacher's Manual, page 31

▶ SPELLING

Hard and Soft c

- Write the following categories on the board or on chart paper: /*s*/ and /*k*/. Mention to students that consonant *c* can have two sounds. Sometimes it sounds like /*s*/, as in *celery* and *recess*. Other times it can sound like /*k*/, as in *candy*, *actor*, and *cattle*. Write each of the words under the correct category. Have students brainstorm other words and add them to each list.

- Have students complete Worktext page 26. Rotating around the small group, ask students to decode and read each of the words found in the Word Bank. Then have them sort the words according to their hard and soft sounds.

- As students complete "Fill in the Blanks," remind them that all of the words can be found in the Word Bank.

CHAPTER 4 LESSON 1 (Part 1)

SPELLING RULE
Words with consonant *c* can have two sounds. Sometimes it sounds like /*k*/, in words such as *camel* or *carpet*. When *c* is followed by an *i*, *e*, or *y*, it sounds like /*s*/, in words such as *center* or *civil*.

A. Say the Words
Say each word in the Word Bank. Remember that consonant *c* sounds like /*s*/ when it is followed by an *i*, *e*, or *y*.

WORD BANK				
coal	city	coin	dice	coat
cat	race	cut	rice	ice
cake	mice	cone	face	

B. Sort the Words
Read the words again in the Word Bank. Sort and write each word under the correct category. Circle the *c* in each word.

/*s*/ /*k*/

_____ _____   _____ _____
_____ _____   _____ _____
_____   _____

C. Fill in the Blanks
Read the sentences and fill in the correct words. The words can be found in the Word Bank. Some sentences may have more than one possible answer.

1. My _____ likes to chase _____.
2. I will _____ down the hill on my bike.
3. The boy has dirt on his _____.
4. The road is a sheet of _____.
5. My _____ is red and white.
6. The _____ cream _____ will taste good.

26 • Chapter 4

Worktext page 26

LESSON 1 (Part 2)

OBJECTIVES

- Students will recognize that consonant *g* can sound hard, like /**g**/, or soft, like /*j*/
- Students will identify words that contain both sounds
- Students will sort words according to their sounds and read sentences to fill in words that have hard *g* and soft *g*

WORD BANK OF REAL WORDS

sugar	gutter	pigeon	arrange	game
gym	page	ago	sage	egg
grid	large	goat	gum	siege
get	huge	rage	gift	age

MATERIALS

Worktext, page 27
Teacher's Manual, page 32

▶ SPELLING

Hard and Soft *g*

- Make two categories on chart paper that say /**g**/ and /*j*/. Explain to students that *g* can sound hard, as in *gutter* or *flag*. Write the two words under /**g**/. Mention that *g* can also sound soft, as in *giraffe* or *orange*. Ask students where they would place *garage*. Tell them that the word contains both sounds, and write it under each category. Have students think of other words that have these sounds. Students can also look up some words in the dictionary to add to the class list.

- Have students turn to page 27 in their Worktexts and complete the spelling page on hard and soft *g*. Help students decode any words they may not be able to read fluently. Coach students as they sort the words according to their sounds.

- Have students complete "Fill in the Blanks."

LESSON 1 (Part 2)

SPELLING RULE
A word with consonant *g* can have two sounds. Sometimes it sounds hard, as in *gutter* or *flag*. When *g* is followed by *i, e,* or *y,* it usually sounds soft, as in *giraffe* or *orange*. There are some exceptions to the rule. For example, if a word has *ge* at the end of it, consonant *g* sounds like /*j*/, as in *gauge*. Or, *g* has a hard sound, as in the word *give*.

A. Say the Words
Say each word in the Word Bank. Remember that consonant *g* usually sounds like /*j*/ when it is followed by *i, e,* or *y.*

WORD BANK				
game	goat	gym	page	siege
sage	huge	egg	gum	gift

B. Sort the Words
Read the words again in the Word Bank. Sort and write each word under the correct category. Circle the *g* in each word.

/g/	/j/
_____	_____
_____	_____
_____	_____
_____	_____

C. Fill in the Blanks
Read the sentences and fill in the correct words. The words can be found in the Word Bank.

1. I like to eat an _____ and toast.
2. The baby likes to play a _____.
3. I like to chew _____.
4. I will give my dad a _____.
5. This _____ of work is easy.
6. I like to play ball in the _____.

Lesson 1 • 27

Worktext page 27

LESSON 1 (Part 3)

OBJECTIVES

- Students will recognize that consonant *y* can also stand for vowels, such as long *e* and long *i*

- Students will identify words containing *y* that have the long *e* and long *i* sounds

- Students will sort words according to their sounds as well as read sentences, identifying the targeted sounds

WORD BANK OF REAL WORDS

fly	sty	family	twenty	baby
try	shy	funny	cry	puppy
dry	my	why	very	
sky	many	by	pretty	

MATERIALS

Worktext, page 28
Teacher's Manual, page 33

▶ SPELLING

Y as a Vowel

Write the following two categories on chart paper or the board: **long *e*, long *i***. Explain to students that *y* can sometimes sound like long *e*, in words such as *family* and *twenty*. Mention that it can also sound like long *i*, in words such as *fly* and *sty*. Have students brainstorm other words that contain these sounds and add them to each category.

- Ask students to turn to page 28 in their Worktexts. Students may need help in decoding some of the words on their list that contain two syllables, such as *baby*, *funny*, *puppy*, *many*, and *pretty*. Rotate around the room, coaching students as they sort their words.

- As students complete "What's the Vowel Sound?" mention that some sentences contain more than one word that contains the targeted sounds. Have them circle words where *y* sounds like long *i*, and underline words where consonant *y* sounds like long *e*.

LESSON 1 (Part 3)

SPELLING RULE
Consonant *y* can stand for vowels, such as long *e* and long *i*, as in the words *family* and *fly*.

A. Say the Words
Say each word in the Word Bank. Remember that y can stand for vowels such as long *e* and long *i*.

WORD BANK

baby	very	sky	try
funny	many	cry	puppy
fly	my	by	pretty

B. Sort the Words
Read the words again in the Word Bank. Sort and write each word under the correct category. Circle the y in each word.

/i/	/e/
_____	_____
_____	_____
_____	_____
_____	_____
_____	

C. What's the Vowel Sound?
Read each sentence. Circle words where consonant y sounds like long *i*. Underline words where consonant y sounds like long *e*.

1. My puppy is shy.
2. The baby will cry when she wakes up.
3. The sky is blue.
4. Tom is so funny.
5. Many of my friends are very funny.
6. I like to fly on a plane.

28 • Chapter 4

Worktext page 28

LESSON 2

OBJECTIVES

- Students will decode and read three-phoneme words that contain initial and final consonant blends
- Students will build and spell words using letter cards
- Students will practice reading by playing a game, completing a crossword puzzle, and unscrambling words containing consonant blends

WORD BANK OF REAL WORDS

free	play	glue	ears	sky
plea	slow	sway	oink	flee
east	ask	elf	act	oats
arch	aunt	alp	elk	arm

MATERIALS

Worktext, pages 29–31
Teacher's Manual, pages 34–35
Assessment Checklist, page 70
Award Certificate, page 71
letter cards for each pair of students

▶ SUBSTITUTION ROUTINES

Initial and Final Consonant Blends

- Write the word **play** on the board. Ask a volunteer to read the word, then have the class write the word down on paper. Explain to students that you will say another word that rhymes with *play*, but you will be substituting the initial consonant blend with two other sounds and letters. Say the word **stay** and ask them to write the word below *play*. Do the same routine with *tray, clay,* and *gray.*
- Repeat this routine with other words in the Word Bank.
- When students are proficient at substituting initial consonant blends to make rhyming words, have them spell other words, such as *arch, elk, ears,* and *oink.* As you say each word, elongate each sound without segmenting it.

▶ SORTING ROUTINES

Initial and Final Consonant Blends

Write each word from the Word Bank on index cards. Have students take turns sorting each word according to the vowel pattern. As students sort, have them read each word aloud.

▶ WORD-BUILDING ROUTINES

- Provide each student or pair of students with a set of letter cards. Determine what words you'd like students to practice making. For example, ask them to pull the following letter cards from their sets: *y, c, d, f, r, l, s, k, t.* Ask them to make as many words as they can, using *y* as a long *i* sound, as in the word *sky.* One student can make a word, then the other can write it down, switching roles after every two words they make.
- You may wish to have students time themselves, then award a certificate to the person or pair who makes the most words in a five-minute time period. The certificate can be found on page 71 of this manual.

▶ PRACTICE

A. Word Race

Have two students play this game, found on Worktext page 29. Remind them that when they think of a rhyming word, the word needs to have the same spelling pattern as the one found in the Word Bank, such as *crew* and *few* for *flew* and *blue* and *cue* for *true.*

B. Crossword Puzzle

Invite students to complete Worktext page 30. As students work on the crossword puzzle, have them cross out words they've used in the Word Bank.

C. Unscramble the Words

Before students unscramble the words found on Worktext page 31, remind them that each word will contain an initial or final consonant blend, such as in the words *fly* and *end.*

Worktext page 29

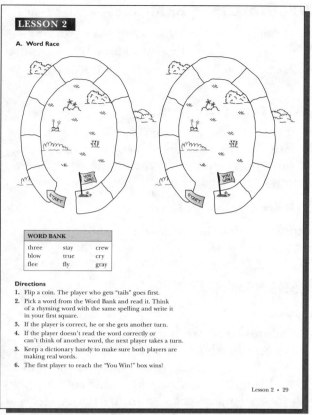

A. Word Race

WORD BANK

three	stay	crew
blow	true	cry
flee	fly	gray

Directions

1. Flip a coin. The player who gets "tails" goes first.
2. Pick a word from the Word Bank and read it. Think of a rhyming word with the same spelling and write it in your first square.
3. If the player is correct, he or she gets another turn.
4. If the player doesn't read the word correctly or can't think of another word, the next player takes a turn.
5. Keep a dictionary handy to make sure both players are making real words.
6. The first player to reach the "You Win!" box wins!

Lesson 2 • 29

Worktext page 31

C. Unscramble the Words

Below is a series of words to unscramble. The first one is done for you. Remember that each word contains either an initial consonant blend, such as *fly*, or a final consonant blend, such as *end*. When you unscramble the word, write it. Then read the word and place a check mark (✓) next to the word, indicating that you read it.

			Write the word.	Read the word.
y	**f**	**l**	fly	☑
1. ew	r	g	_____	☐
2. a	ch	r	_____	☐
3. t	ay	s	_____	☐
4. ue	l	c	_____	☐
5. au	t	n	_____	☐
6. t	a	c	_____	☐
7. ea	t	s	_____	☐
8. r	t	ue	_____	☐
9. ee	r	f	_____	☐
10. g	ue	l	_____	☐
11. ow	l	p	_____	☐
12. y	t	r	_____	☐
13. g	ow	l	_____	☐
14. ew	s	t	_____	☐
15. r	t	a	_____	☐
16. gr	l	ow	_____	☐
17. m	th	a	_____	☐
18. th	ee	r	_____	☐
19. oa	s	t	_____	☐
20. m	r	a	_____	☐

Lesson 2 • 31

Worktext page 30

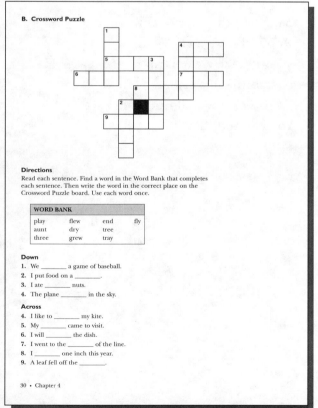

B. Crossword Puzzle

Directions

Read each sentence. Find a word in the Word Bank that completes each sentence. Then write the word in the correct place on the Crossword Puzzle board. Use each word once.

WORD BANK

play	flew	end	fly
aunt	dry	tree	
three	grew	tray	

Down

1. We _____ a game of baseball.
2. I put food on a _____.
3. I ate _____ nuts.
4. The plane _____ in the sky.

Across

4. I like to _____ my kite.
5. My _____ came to visit.
6. I will _____ the dish.
7. I went to the _____ of the line.
8. I _____ one inch this year.
9. A leaf fell off the _____.

30 • Chapter 4

LESSON 3

OBJECTIVES

- Students will apply their decoding skills by reading newspaper articles containing three-sound, initial, and final consonants
- Students will apply their comprehension skills by writing sentences about the *who, what, when, where,* and *why* of one article
- Students will read and identify initial and final consonant blends
- Students will create their own class newspaper based on events that occur in their school

MATERIALS

Worktext, pages 32–35
Teacher's Manual, pages 36–37
Award Certificate, page 71

▶ DECODING AND READING

A. Food Drive

Before having students read the school newspaper article, help them to decode the following words: *homeless, people, Friday.* Point out that the word *homeless* is a compound word, made up of two smaller words. Cover up *home* and have them decode *less.* Then cover up *less* so they can read *home.* Finally, have them read the compound word.

B. Who? What? When? Where? Why?

Ask students to reread the article. Then have them answer questions pertaining to the action in the article. Encourage them to write one or two sentences about the *who, what, when, where,* and *why* of the article.

C. School News

Have students read the articles from Room 101. Point out any words that might give them difficulty in decoding. If they stumble over *Friday, Saturday,* and *Thursday,* write the days of the week on the board. Add any important words that students need to know, so they can become familiar with them.

D. Where Are the Consonant Blends?

Have students read the small article on Worktext page 35. Then ask them to find and circle six initial and final consonant blends. Ask them to write and read each word aloud.

E. Write Your Own Article

Assist students in writing their own articles about important class or school events or bits of news that they would find interesting. Invite a student to input the articles and create a class newspaper.

F. Write a Get-Well Note

Encourage students to write a get-well note to a classmate, friend, or family member.

▶ ASSESSMENT

Dictation

Have students write down each sentence as you dictate it. Say the sentence a few times before having them write. When they're ready, say each sentence slowly and clearly. If students have difficulty thinking of how to spell a particular word, have them leave a blank or write as much of the word as they can.

1. We will have a food drive.
2. Bring a can of food to class.
3. Sal made the swim team.
4. Rob will have a car wash.
5. We will take a class trip in May.
6. Nick broke his arm.
7. Pat is sick and will not be in class.
8. You can send Pat a note.

LESSON 3

A. Food Drive
Read the following article about a food drive.

> **We Need Your Help!**
> **...from Room 101**
>
> We need your help! Cody, Jane, Ned, and Kate will have a food drive for the homeless people in the city. They ask that each of you get one can of food from home. You can drop it off on Friday in Room 101. If each of you can give us one can of food, we will feed 100 people. We want to help the homeless in the city. We need your help too!

Worktext page 32

B. Who? What? When? Where? Why?
Reread the article about the food drive. Then answer the following five questions. Write one or two sentences explaining the *who, what, when, where,* and *why* of the article.

1. **Who** is doing the action? _____
   _____
   _____
   _____

2. **What** are they doing? _____
   _____
   _____
   _____

3. **When** are they doing it? _____
   _____
   _____
   _____

4. **Where** are they doing it? _____
   _____
   _____
   _____

5. **Why** are they doing it? _____
   _____
   _____
   _____

Worktext page 33

C. School News
Read the following articles.

> **The News...from Room 101**
>
> - Sal, Jose, Kate, and Tom made the swim team. They will have a swim meet on Friday at 3:00 P.M. Come cheer them on!
>
> - Jay, Rob, and Maria will have a car wash on Saturday. If you can come and help, go to the lot at the back of the school. Come at 9:00 A.M. The cash that we make will go to a class trip that we will take in May.
>
> - Nick broke his arm at the track meet last week. He will help Coach Mead until his cast is off.
>
> - Pat is sick and will be back to class next week. If you like, you can send her a get-well note. You can send it to:
>
>   Pat Van Fleet
>   35 Pine Cone Road
>   Oak Park, CA 91206
>
> - Jan and Brad will sing at the class play on Thursday.

Worktext page 34

D. Where Are the Consonant Blends?
Read the article below. Find six words that contain two consonants next to each other that make two different sounds, such as **sw**im, **cl**ass, se**nd**, or la**st**. Circle each word that you find. Then write the words below the article.

> Nick broke his arm at the track meet last week. He will help Coach Mead until his cast is off.

1. _____   4. _____
2. _____   5. _____
3. _____   6. _____

E. Write Your Own Article
Think of something that will happen or has happened in your school or class. Write a short article about it. Collect articles from other students and type them on a computer. Make up your own class newspaper.

_____
_____
_____
_____
_____

F. Write a Get-Well Note
Reread the article about Pat Van Fleet, a student from Room 101 who is sick. Then write her a get-well note. Or, if someone is sick in your class, write a note to cheer him or her up!

Dear _____,

_____
_____

Sincerely,

_____

Worktext page 35

CHAPTER 5
Four-Sound Words

TOKEN LESSON A

OBJECTIVES
- Students will develop phonemic awareness as they use tokens to segment nonsense words comprised of four sounds that include initial and consonant blends
- Students will discriminate sounds through substitution and deletion routines as well as shifting the position of sounds

WORD BANK OF NONSENSE WORDS

krig	skaj	stuv	twim	slig
gesp	lusk	moft	tainz	dift
inst	umps	akst	olpt	ilps
frud	ploe	naft	sieks	onts

WORD BANK OF REAL WORDS

swim	desk	prow	stub	tusk
gasp	loft	task	soft	last
plow	plot	bump	musk	brim
raft	mask	twin	dump	jump

MATERIALS
Teacher's Manual, pages 38–39
token cards
additional list of nonsense words, page 72

▶ PHONEMIC AWARENESS

Segmenting Sounds

Place four tokens on the table, such as a star, triangle, circle, and square.

- Say it slowly: *Krig.* **What is the first sound you hear in** *krig*? As you say the word whole, elongating each sound, have a student point to the star and say / k /.

- Say it slowly: *Krig.* **What is the second sound you hear in** *krig*? Ask a student to say the word, stretching each sound. Cut the student off after saying / r /. Ask the student to point to the token that stands for that sound. (*the triangle*)

- Say it slowly: *Krig.* **What is the third sound you hear in** *krig*? The student says the word slowly and focuses on what comes after the / r /. When the student identifies / i /, have the student point to the circle.

- Say it slowly: *Krig.* **What is the last sound you hear in** *krig*? Have the student say / g / and point to the square.

- Rotating around the small group, invite other students to segment and sound out nonsense words from the Word Bank.

k   r   i   g

▶ WORD-PAIR ROUTINES

Consonant Blends

Place a diamond, circle, and star on the table.

- Say: **This says** *kaj.* **I'm going to make** *skaj.* Add a rectangle before the diamond and circle. Say: **What new sound did I add?** Invite a student to say / s / and point to the rectangle.

- Repeat this routine with other nonsense words containing initial consonant blends.

- Put a rectangle, circle, and square on the table. Say: **This says** *mot.* **I'm going to make** *moft.* Add a diamond in between the circle and square. Ask a volunteer to say the added sound (/ f /) and point to the new token representing that sound.

- Place a star, circle, and diamond in front of students. Say: **This says** *olp.* **I'm going to make** *olpt.* Put a square at the end of the nonsense word and invite a student to say the added sound / t /. Have students segment each sound, elongating and emphasizing each of the three consonant sounds in the second, third, and fourth positions.

- Once students have worked with CCVC, CVCC, and VCCC patterns, invite them to make new nonsense words. Say: **If this says** *ums*, **make** *umps*. Students should be able to place a new token in between the second and third sounds, and identify the added sound / p /.

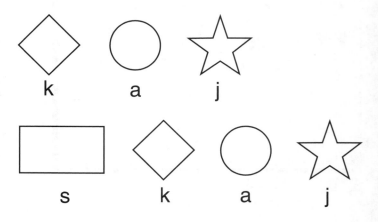

k   a   j

s   k   a   j

▶ SUBSTITUTION ROUTINES

Initial Consonant Blends

On the table, place a triangle, diamond, circle, and square.

- Say: **If this says *stuv*, make *smuv*.** Invite a volunteer to replace the diamond with another token. Ask the student to sound out the new nonsense word.

- Have students substitute other consonants to form new nonsense words, such as *slig/srig*, *frud/flud*, and *ploe/proe*.

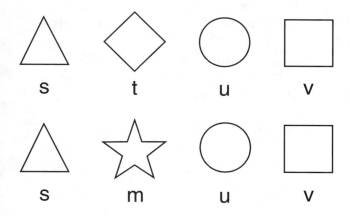

Final Consonant Blends

- Use new tokens and have students substitute consonants in the third and fourth positions, such as *dift/difs*, *lusk/lumk*, and *gesp/gesk*.

- As a challenge, invite students to substitute tokens to create new nonsense words containing three consonants, such as *akst/amst/amsk*.

▶ SHIFTING ROUTINES

When students are proficient at substituting initial and final consonant blends, introduce a nonsense word and shift the position of sounds within that particular word.

- Place a rectangle, circle, triangle, and star on the table. Say: **If this says *slig*, make *ligs*.** Guide a student while shifting the rectangle from the first position to the fourth position.

- Say: **If this says *ligs*, make *glis*.** Invite a volunteer to shift positions by moving the star to the first position.

- Say: **If this says *glis*, make *ilgs*.** After shifting positions, placing the triangle, circle, star, and rectangle in a row, have the student point to each token to segment the nonsense word.

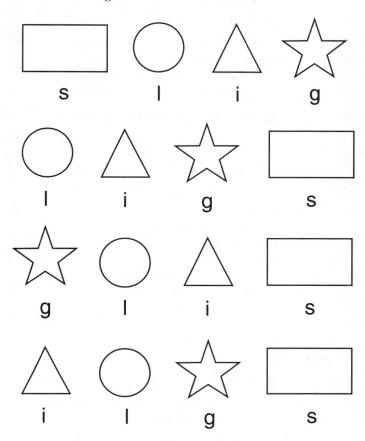

- If students have trouble with these, try *skree/krees/reeks/reesk*.

- For additional four-sound nonsense words containing initial and final consonant blends, turn to page 72.

- After students have worked with four-sound nonsense words, you can use the Word Bank of Real Words with them.

TOKEN LESSON B

OBJECTIVES

- Students will segment four-sound words comprised of initial or final consonant blends by connecting sounds to letters

- Students will make and then read new nonsense words by adding, substituting, deleting, or shifting the position of letters

WORD BANK OF NONSENSE WORDS

brosh	snij	gliz	speg	troep
fiapt	dind	tanz	luft	chuvz
umps	elfth	reps	frak	soild
sploe	klech	pras	twoit	sweeth

MATERIALS

Teacher's Manual, pages 40–41
Assessment Checklist, page 70
token cards
letter cards, including all vowels, vowel pairs, consonants, and consonant digraphs

▶ PHONICS

Connecting Sounds to Letters

Place three different-shaped tokens on the table. Keep a set of letter cards handy.

- Say it slowly: **Brosh.** Point to the first token and say: **What sound does this make?** After a student responds /b/, say: **Find the letter that makes that sound.** Invite the student to place the letter b under the first token.

- Say it slowly: **Brosh.** Point to the second token and say: **What sound does this make?** Have the student place the letter r below the second token and say /r/.

- Say it slowly: **Brosh.** Point to the third token and say: **What sound does this make?** As the student says /o/, ask the student to point to the token representing that sound.

- Say it slowly: **Brosh.** Point to the last token and say: **What sound does this make?** Coach the student to find the consonant digraph letter card that says /sh/.

- Using other nonsense words found in the Word Bank, repeat this routine with all of your students. Be sure to practice words containing initial and final consonant blends.

▶ SUBSTITUTION ROUTINES

Initial Consonant Blends

Once students are able to identify and connect the sounds to letters, remove the tokens and manipulate the letter cards only. Explain that you're going to substitute consonants in the first and second position of each nonsense word.

- Say: **If this says *snij*, make *slij*.** Say the word slowly, emphasizing and elongating the first two consonant sounds. Coach a volunteer to find the letter *l* to replace the *n*.

- Say: **If this says *slij*, make *prij*.** Ask students how many sounds have been changed, coaching them to substitute *sl* with *pr*.

- Repeat this routine with other nonsense words until all students have had the opportunity to manipulate the letter cards.

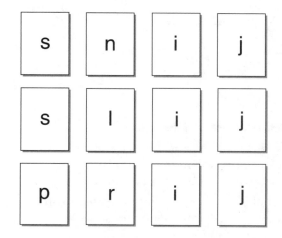

Final Consonant Blends

Mention to students that you will be substituting consonants at the end of each nonsense word. Ask them to listen carefully for those sounds.

- Say: **If this says *chuvz*, make *chuvd*.** Have a student substitute the last consonant for the letter *d*.

- Say: **If this says *chuvd*, make *chuvg*.** Have a volunteer substitute the last consonant for the letter *g*.

- Say: **If this says *chuvg*, make *chuvth*.** Invite a student to substitute *th* for *g*.

- Rotate around the small group as students work with substituting final consonant blends.

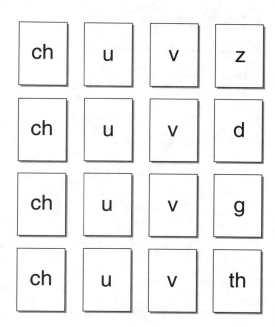

▶ DELETION ROUTINES

Explain to students that you will be deleting a consonant somewhere in each nonsense word. Ask them to listen carefully as you elongate each sound, without segmenting the word.

- Say: **If this says** *twoit,* **make** *toit.* Have the student remove the *w,* and say the new nonsense word.
- Repeat this routine with other nonsense words, such as *soild/ soid, pras/ pas, elfth/ elth,* and *sploe/ spoe.*

▶ SHIFTING ROUTINES

As you begin the next routine, mention that you will be shifting the position of letters within each word. Because this is a more challenging activity, stretch each sound as you say the nonsense word.

- Say: **If this says** *klech,* **make** *chelk.* Encourage a volunteer to shift the initial consonant /k/ with the final consonant digraph /ch/, as well as shifting the position of the *e* and *l.*

- Continue the routine and have students make other nonsense words, such as *kelch.*

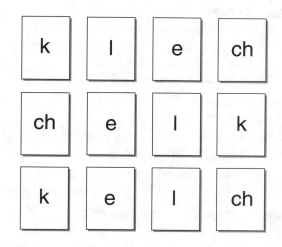

▶ READING ROUTINES

Blending Sounds

After students have practiced manipulating and spelling nonsense words, assess their ability to read the words that they are making.

Place the word *umps* in front of a student and invite him or her to read it. If read correctly, ask the next student to read a new nonsense word.

▶ INFORMAL ASSESSMENT

Use the Assessment Checklist found on page 70 to determine whether students are able to decode and read four-sound nonsense words that contain either initial or final consonant blends.

LESSON 1 (Part 1)

OBJECTIVES

- Students will recognize that words with *kn*, *wr*, *gn*, and *mb* stand for only one sound. One of the consonants is silent, as in *know*, *write*, *sign*, and *lamb*
- Students will identify words containing silent letters
- Students will sort words according to their spelling pattern
- Students will read sentences, fill in the correct word, and identify misspelled words

WORD BANK OF REAL WORDS

knit	knob	sign	write	wrist
wreck	limb	know	climb	thumb
kneel	comb	gnaw	lamb	wrench
wren	design	knife	knot	wrap

MATERIALS

Worktext, page 36
Teacher's Manual, page 42

CHAPTER 5 LESSON 1 (Part 1)

SPELLING RULE
Words with *kn, wr, gn,* and *mb* stand for only one sound. One of the consonants is silent, as in *know, write, sign,* and *lamb.*

A. Say the Words
Say each word in the Word Bank. Remember that one of the consonants in each word is silent.

WORD BANK

knit	knob	sign	write	wrist
wreck	limb	know	climb	thumb
kneel	comb	gnaw	lamb	wrench
wren	design	knife		

B. Sort the Words
Read the words again in the Word Bank. Sort and write each word under the correct category. Circle the silent letter in each word.

kn	wr	gn	mb

C. Proofread the Note
Read the note that Jen sent to her Aunt Sue. Find the five misspelled words and underline them. Write them correctly on the lines below.

Dear Aunt Sue,

Thank you for the get-well note. My rist and thum feel better. When I can, I will nit you a sweater made of wool from a lam. Please rite back.

Love,
Jen

1. _____ 2. _____ 3. _____ 4. _____ 5. _____

36 • Chapter 5

Worktext page 36

▶ SPELLING

Kn, wr, gn, mb

- Write the following categories on the board: **kn**, **wr**, **gn**, and **mb**. Explain to students that each of these consonant pairs represents one sound, and in each pair, one consonant is silent. Write the following words below the correct categories: **know**, **write**, **sign**, and **lamb**.

- Rotating around the room, have students read each of the words found in the Word Bank, on Worktext page 36. Then ask students to sort the words according to their consonant pairs.

- As students proofread the note from Jen to Aunt Sue, mention that the correct spelling of words can be found in the Word Bank.

LESSON 1 (Part 2)

OBJECTIVES

- Students will recognize the sounds *r*-controlled vowels make. For example, the vowel sound in *far* can be spelled *ar*. The vowel sound in *forth* can be spelled *or*. And the vowel sound in *bird* can be spelled *ir*, *er*, and *ur*, as in *fir*, *her*, and *burn*

- Students will identify words containing *r*-controlled vowels

- Students will sort words according to their vowel sounds and identify words in sentences containing these sounds

WORD BANK OF REAL WORDS

far	forth	bird	fir	her
burn	car	girl	large	shore
form	hurt	first	church	
skirt	turn	nerve	thirst	
verb	serve	storm	march	
corn	hard	sport	germ	

MATERIALS

Worktext, page 37
Teacher's Manual, page 43

▶ **SPELLING**

R-controlled Vowels

- Write the following categories on the board: **ar**, **or**, **ir**, **er**, and **ur**. Explain to students that the vowel sound in *far* can be spelled *ar*, while the vowel sound in *forth* can be spelled *or*. Mention that the sound in *bird* can be spelled *ir*, *er*, and *ur*, as in *fir*, *her*, and *burn*. Ask students to think of words they know that end in those sounds. Have volunteers write each of the words under the correct category on the board. Invite them to think of other words where the *r* controls the vowel sound.

- Have students turn to page 37 in the Worktext. Ask volunteers to read each word aloud. Then have them work individually, sorting the words according to their sound and spelling pattern.

- As students complete "What's the Vowel Sound?" have them circle words that contain a vowel followed by *r*. Remind them that there may be more than one word in each sentence to circle.

LESSON 1 (Part 2)

SPELLING RULE
The vowel sound in *far* can be spelled *ar*. The vowel sound in *forth* can be spelled *or*. The vowel sound in *bird* can be spelled *ir*, *er*, and *ur*, as in *fir*, *her*, and *burn*.

A. Say the Words
Say each word in the Word Bank and listen for the vowel sound with *r*.

WORD BANK				
car	girl	large	shore	form
hurt	first	church	skirt	turn
nerve	thirst	verb	serve	storm
march	corn	hard	sport	germ

B. Sort the Words
Read the words again in the Word Bank. Sort and write each word under the correct category. Circle the vowel plus *r*.

ar	or	er	ir	ur

C. What's the Vowel Sound?
Read each sentence. Circle words that contain a vowel followed by *r*.

1. I drove my car through the storm.
2. First, we went to the shore.
3. Jay will pick corn in the large field.
4. Her skirt is red and white.
5. Please turn left at the stop sign.
6. The class will form a line.
7. I lost my nerve at the game.
8. The church is on the right.

Lesson 1 · 37

Worktext page 37

LESSON 1 (Part 3)

OBJECTIVES

- Students will recognize that words with *ch*, *tch*, and *ng* stand for one consonant sound, and that words with *nk* stand for two consonant sounds

- Students will identify words containing *ch*, *tch*, *ng*, and *nk*

- Students will sort words according to their sounds and read sentences to fill in words containing these sounds

WORD BANK OF REAL WORDS

much	hatch	ring	rink
watch	think	sing	church
pink	long	pitch	march
wrong	drink	which	crutch
reach	song	thank	catch

MATERIALS

Worktext, page 38
Teacher's Manual, page 44

LESSON 1 (Part 3)

SPELLING RULE
Words with *ch* and *tch* can stand for one-consonant sound, as in *much* and *hatch*. Words with *ng* can stand for one-consonant sound, as in *ring*. Words with *nk* can stand for two-consonant sounds, as in *rink*.

A. Say the Words
Say each word in the Word Bank. Remember that *ch*, *tch*, and *ng* can stand for one sound, and *nk* can stand for two sounds.

WORD BANK

watch	think	sing	reach
pink	long	pitch	march
wrong	drink	which	catch

B. Sort the Words
Read the words again in the Word Bank. Sort and write each word under the correct category. Circle *ch*, *tch*, *ng*, or *nk* in each of the words.

ch	tch	ng	nk
_____	_____	_____	_____
_____	_____	_____	_____
_____	_____	_____	_____

C. Fill in the Blanks
Read the sentences and fill in the correct words. The words can be found in the Word Bank.

1. Jess will _____ first in the game.

2. _____ student would like to sing last?

3. Will you play _____ with me?

4. My shirt is _____.

D. Name That Word
Make words, using *ch*, *tch*, *ng*, or *nk*. You can make words not found in the Word Bank. Use a dictionary to check your answers.

1. si __ __   3. mar __ __   5. dri __ __   7. thi __ __
2. pi __ __ __   4. wro __ __   6. whi __ __   8. ri __ __

38 • Chapter 5

Worktext page 38

▶ SPELLING

Ch, tch, ng, nk

- Chart the following categories on the board: **ch**, **tch**, **ng**, and **nk**. Explain to students that words with *ch*, *tch*, and *ng* stand for one consonant sound, while *nk* has two consonant sounds. When you put a *k* after an *n*, the *n* really sounds like an *ngk*. Say each word slowly and invite volunteers to write them below the correct category: **much**, **hatch**, **ring**, **rink**.

- Rotating around the room, ask students to read each word found in the Word Bank on Worktext page 38. Then have students sort each word according to its sound and spelling pattern.

- Coach students who need additional assistance in completing "Fill in the Blanks" and "Name That Word."

LESSON 2

OBJECTIVES

- Students will decode, read, and sort four-phoneme words that contain initial and final consonant blends
- Students will write lists of rhyming words
- Students will build and spell words using letter cards
- Students will play Word Search and Bingo games, identifying and reading four-sound words

WORD BANK OF REAL WORDS

sleep	zest	mound	kind
skirt	class	stick	swing
bench	barge	brain	frown
court	swell	crowd	bind
drain	drown	quail	swerve

MATERIALS

Worktext, pages 39–41
Teacher's Manual, pages 45–46
Assessment Checklist, page 70
Award Certificate, page 71
letter cards for each pair of students

▶ RHYMING ROUTINES

- Write the word **mound** on the board and say it slowly, so that students hear each of the four sounds. Have them write the word on paper and ask them to brainstorm other words that rhyme with it, changing the initial consonant, as in *bound, found, hound, pound, round, sound,* and *wound.* If a volunteer says *ground,* guide students in writing all five letters. Say the word slowly, stretching the initial consonant blend, **gr**. Repeat this routine with other words found in the Word Bank.

- Invite individuals to come up to the board and spell words that you dictate from the Word Bank. Ask other students to write rhyming words beneath each one. Help students sound out and spell words that contain more than four sounds: *brain/sprain, swing/string.*

▶ SORTING ROUTINES

Write each word from the Word Bank on index cards. Have students take turns sorting each word according to initial or final consonant blends. As students sort, ask them to read each word aloud. Mention that there may be words that don't fit either category.

▶ WORD-BUILDING ROUTINES

- Provide individuals or pairs of students with a set of letter cards. Depending on what spelling pattern students need to practice, ask them to pull specific cards. For example, to work with four-sound words containing /ou/ or /ow/, use the following cards: *b, d, f, g, m, n, o, p, r, s, u, w.* Ask them to make as many words as they can.

- Time students in the word-building activity, then award a certificate to the individual or pair that makes the most words in a five-minute time period. Be sure that the students can read each word correctly. The certificate can be found on page 71.

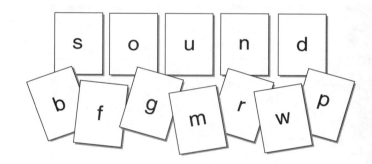

▶ PRACTICE

A. Word-Search Board

Have students complete the Word-Search Board, found on Worktext page 39. Before completing the activity, ask students to take turns reading aloud the words found in the Word Bank.

B. Bingo

Choose a more able reader to be the caller. Have the caller read words from the Word Bank as three other students play the game. Coach students if they have difficulty in identifying words on their Bingo cards.

Worktext page 39

LESSON 2

A. Word-Search Board

On the Word-Search Board below, there are 24 hidden words. As you find each word, read it, then circle it. Words can go across, down, diagonally, or backward. Cross the word out in the Word Bank below.

WORD BANK

sleep	glass	frame	smell	stain
desk	trick	gasp	proud	brown
sound	cling	clown	kind	trail
mind	wrench	kneel	climb	sign
skirt	large	sport	hurt	

G	H	S	M	E	L	L	K	C	I	R	T
O	N	L	I	A	R	T	Q	S	K	T	P
F	D	E	S	K	G	S	C	L	I	M	B
R	S	E	P	T	L	C	L	I	N	G	G
A	S	P	S	V	A	T	O	H	D	A	N
M	K	Y	O	D	S	I	W	A	W	S	W
E	I	F	U	R	S	C	N	J	R	P	O
X	R	N	N	E	T	R	U	H	E	X	R
Q	T	U	D	K	N	E	E	L	N	C	B
L	A	R	G	E	H	R	V	U	C	S	A
V	D	U	O	R	P	Y	D	J	H	I	E

Worktext page 40

B. Bingo

Directions:

1. Each player takes some tokens.

2. Pick a caller.

3. The caller reads a word from the Word Bank in any order.

4. The players put a token on the square that contains the word.

5. The first player to get all of the tokens in a row says, "Bingo!"

WORD BANK

comb	creep	train	stick	crowd
found	last	wreck	thing	stale
find	bench	serve	grass	long
wheel	patch	blink	groom	plain
first	storm	shirt	star	next

Bingo Card I

comb	wreck	find	blink
stale	serve	long	shirt
crowd	first	storm	creep
wheel	groom	train	thing

Worktext page 41

Bingo Card 2

creep	serve	grass	wreck
found	long	plain	next
stale	patch	train	crowd
last	find	wheel	blink

Bingo Card 3

stick	stale	comb	patch
grass	found	first	star
bench	creep	plain	shirt
train	find	wheel	last

LESSON 3

OBJECTIVES
- Students will apply their decoding skills by reading directions to a game, an invitation, and a newspaper advertisement
- Students will apply their writing skills by writing directions from school to home, writing an invitation, and writing a newspaper advertisement
- Students will read and identify four-sound words

MATERIALS
Worktext, pages 42–45
Teacher's Manual, pages 47–49
Award Certificate, page 71

▶ DECODING AND READING

A. Directions to the Game

- Before having students read Worktext page 42, write the following word on the board: **front**. Explain to students that the word contains five sounds and two consonant blends, *fr* and *nt*. Say the word slowly, elongating each sound, but still blending them together. Invite a volunteer to segment the sounds, then blend them together to form the word.

- Write other words on the board that students may have difficulty decoding, such as **driveway**. Tell them that the word is a compound word comprised of two words they already know. Help them decode it by covering up *way* and reading *drive*. Then cover up *drive* and read *way*. Invite a volunteer to read the two words together to form the compound word.

B. The Post-Game Party

Have students read the invitation silently, and then ask them to practice reading it a few times. Time their reading of the invitation, encouraging them to read it as fluently as possible. Award a certificate to those students who have made the most progress recently. See page 71 for the certificate.

C. Find the Consonant Blends

Ask students to reread the directions found on page 43 in their Worktexts. Tell them that each direction line contains one or more words that have initial or final consonant blends. Have them read the directions silently, and circle the words containing the blends. Mention that there may be words that contain both an initial and final consonant blend.

D. Make Up Your Own Directions

Before completing this writing activity, ask students to think of how they would give directions to a friend if they were going from school to the local movie theater. As students tell you each direction line, write it on the board. Then ask them to write directions from school to their own homes.

Teacher Tip

If . . . students have difficulty writing some of the words in their directions, tell them to leave a space or draw a blank line.

Then . . . have them come back to that direction when they're done with the activity. You can help them by asking them to sound out the word, segmenting each sound and writing each letter that they hear, until they have written the entire word.

E. Party Time!

Have students write an invitation to a party they'd like to have, filling in the particulars of *when, time, place,* and what they'd like their guests to *bring*.

F. First Come! First Served!

Before reading the newspaper advertisement, write the following words on the board: **skirt**, **slack**, **belt**, and **band**. Mention that all of the words contain four sounds, inviting volunteers to read each word. Then add an *s* to the end of each word, saying that each word now contains five sounds. Have students read the words, adding */s/* to the end of each.

G. Half-Off Sale! Come While It Lasts!

Invite students to write an advertisement telling about a half-off sale at their own clothing store. Ask them to come up with a title for the advertisement, the name of their store, and a brief description of the sale. Using the Word Bank and other words they know, have them list the clothing items, the original price, and the half-off price.

▶ ASSESSMENT

Dictation

Have students write down each sentence as you dictate it. Say the sentence a few times before having them write. When they're ready, say each sentence slowly and distinctly. If students have difficulty thinking of how to spell a particular word, have them leave a blank or write as much of the word as possible.

1. All cars can form a line next to the curb.
2. Make a left on Pine Trail Road.
3. Turn into the large lot.
4. Join the team in a post-game party.
5. All price tags will say "half off."
6. We will sell three skirts.
7. Two sweatbands are for sale.
8. I sold a pair of blue jeans.

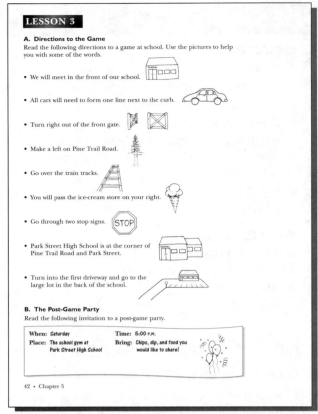

Worktext page 42

Worktext page 43

F. First Come! First Served!

Read the newspaper advertisement below.

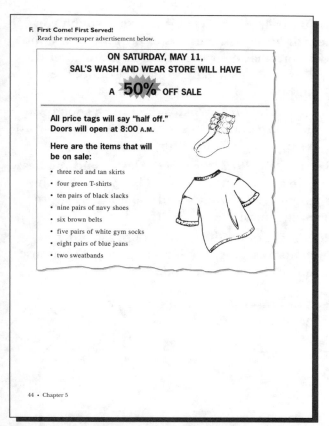

**ON SATURDAY, MAY 11,
SAL'S WASH AND WEAR STORE WILL HAVE**

A **50%** OFF SALE

All price tags will say "half off."
Doors will open at 8:00 A.M.

**Here are the items that will
be on sale:**

- three red and tan skirts
- four green T-shirts
- ten pairs of black slacks
- nine pairs of navy shoes
- six brown belts
- five pairs of white gym socks
- eight pairs of blue jeans
- two sweatbands

Worktext page 44

G. Half-Off Sale! Come While It Lasts!

Pretend that you own your own clothing store. What would you sell? How much would it cost? Suppose you had a "half-off" sale. How much would each item cost then? Write a newspaper advertisement telling about the sale. Make a list of the items that are for sale. Write the price next to each and then the half-off price. Use your Word Bank for items you might like to sell. Think of other items and add them to your list.

WORD BANK			
skirt	shirts	slacks	shoes
belts	socks	jeans	sweat bands

Title of Advertisement: _____

_____

_____

_____

Sale Items: **Price:**   **Half-Off Price:**

_____

_____

_____

_____

_____

_____

_____

Worktext page 45

CHAPTER 6
Five- and Six-Sound Words

TOKEN LESSON A

OBJECTIVES
- Students will develop phonemic awareness as they use tokens to segment five- and six-sound nonsense words that include initial and final consonant blends
- Students will discriminate sounds through substitution and deletion routines as well as through shifting the position of sounds in nonsense words

WORD BANK OF NONSENSE WORDS

plift	gloaft	baulps	throinch
thelkt	scrome	lowkst	flauts
skurbd	kroifs	vults	shiemps
snimps	stroilsh	proimst	troulks
kipst	bonts	fencht	skunsht

WORD BANK OF REAL WORDS

plank	crisp	springs
skimps	splint	bunts
claps	streets	trusts
clasp	strict	stump

MATERIALS
Teacher's Manual, pages 50–51
token cards
additional list of nonsense words, page 72

▶ PHONEMIC AWARENESS

Segmenting Sounds

Place five tokens in front of a small group of students, such as a circle, square, triangle, star, and diamond.

- Say it slowly: *Plift*. **What is the first sound you hear in *plift*?** As you stretch out each sound, be sure to emphasize each phoneme, especially the initial and final consonant blends. Invite volunteers to point to the circle and say /p/.

- Say it slowly: *Plift*. **What is the second sound you hear in *plift*?** Ask students to sound out the non-sense word, stopping them after the /l/. Have them isolate that sound and point to the token that corresponds to it. (*square*)

- Say it slowly: *Plift*. **What is the third sound you hear in *plift*?** Ask students to say *plift* slowly and focus on what their mouths are making after the /l/. As students make the short *i* sound, they should point to the triangle.

- Say it slowly: *Plift*. **What is the fourth sound you hear in *plift*?** Students should sound out the word and stop after /f/, pointing to the star.

- Say it slowly: *Plift*. **What is the last sound you hear in *plift*?** Have students say /t/ and point to the diamond. Ask them to read the nonsense word, blending all of the sounds together.

- Rotating around the small group, ask other students to segment five- and six-sound nonsense words from the Word Bank.

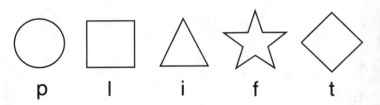

▶ SUBSTITUTION ROUTINES

Place a diamond, star, rectangle, circle, and triangle on the table.

- Say: **If this says *gloaft*, make *gloath*.** Coach a student in taking away the circle and triangle and replacing them with a square.

- Have students substitute other sounds to form new nonsense words, such as *snimps/shimps/thimps*; *flauts/flauth/flauch*; *bonts/bants/banth*; *vults/thults/chults*.

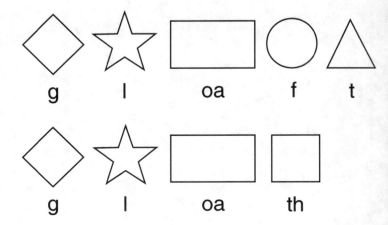

▶ DELETION ROUTINES

On the table, place a circle, square, triangle, star, diamond, and rectangle.

- Say: **This says *proimst*. Make *poimst*.** Invite a student to remove the square, deleting /r/ from the nonsense word.

- Say: **This says *poimst*. Make *poimt*.** Guide the student in removing the diamond or /s/ from the nonsense word.

- Say: **This says *poimt*. Make *oimt*.** The student should now delete the circle or /p/ from the word.

- Say: **This says *oimt*. Make *oit*.** As the student hears that the /m/ is omitted from the word, he or she should remove the star.

- Have students work with other nonsense words from the Word Bank, deleting phonemes step by step.

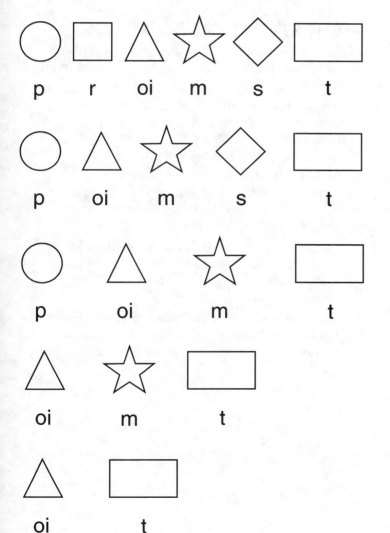

▶ SHIFTING ROUTINES

When students are able to substitute and delete phonemes with ease, challenge them to shift the position of sounds in nonsense words. Place a star, circle, square, triangle, and diamond on the table.

- Say: **If this says *kroifs*, make *roifsk*.** Watch as students shift the star to the last position.

- Say: **If this says *roifsk*, make *froisk*.** Guide students to shift the triangle and circle into the first and second positions.

- Repeat this routine with other nonsense words.

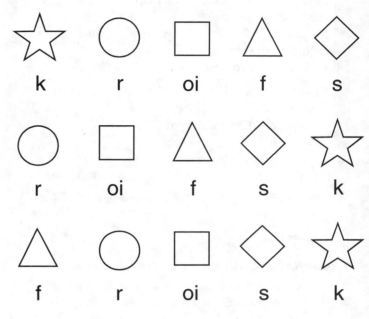

- For additional five- and six-sound words, turn to page 72.

- After students have worked with five- and six-sound nonsense words, you can use the Word Bank of Real Words with them.

TOKEN LESSON B

OBJECTIVES
- Students will segment five- and six-sound nonsense words, some comprised of two and three initial and final consonant blends
- Students will make and then read new nonsense words by adding, substituting, deleting, or shifting the position of letters

WORD BANK OF NONSENSE WORDS

klingk	spleef	naimps	gompt
prensk	blaimst	skloop	krumst
strangk	gleend	thwomps	flamst
stowpst	skreefs	swivz	snumd
sploibd	splawps	bloorch	kwanst
trolch	drowpths	twonch	frelk

MATERIALS
Teacher's Manual, pages 52–53
Assessment Checklist, page 70
token cards
letter cards, including all vowels, vowel pairs, consonants, and consonant digraphs

▶ PHONICS

Connecting Sounds to Letters

Place five different tokens on the table, such as a diamond, star, circle, square, and triangle.

- Say it slowly: *Twonch.* Point to the first token and say: **What sound does this make?** After a student responds /t/, say: **Find the letter that makes that sound.** Have the student find the letter t and place it beneath the diamond.
- Say it slowly: *Twonch.* Point to the second token and say: **What sound does this make?** Have the student say /w/ and place the letter card beneath the star.
- Say it slowly: *Twonch.* Point to the third token and say: **What sound does this make?** After the student says /o/, he or she should place the corresponding letter card beneath the circle.

- Say it slowly: *Twonch.* Point to the fourth token and say: **What sound does this make?** The student should say /n/ and place the letter card below the square.
- Say it slowly: *Twonch.* Point to the last token and say: **What sound does this make?** Coach the student to look for the consonant digraph /ch/ and place that letter card beneath the triangle.
- Using other five- and six-sound nonsense words from the Word Bank, have students connect the sounds to letters using the cards.

Teacher Tip
Pay special attention to nonsense words containing three-sound consonant blends, as in *sploibd, strangk,* or *splawps.* Be sure to stretch the sounds so students can discriminate each one.

▶ SUBSTITUTION ROUTINES
Once students are able to connect the sounds to letters, remove the tokens and work with the letter cards only.

- Say: **If this says *prensk*, make *brensk*.** Say the word slowly, especially elongating the initial and final consonant blends. Guide a volunteer in substituting the letter p with the letter b.
- Say: **If this says *brensk*, make *breensk*.** Coach a student to substitute the letters ee for e, which now makes the nonsense word have a long-vowel sound.
- Say: **If this says *breensk*, make *breensh*.** Be sure that when the student substitutes the letters s and k with sh, he or she pronounces /sh/ as one sound, not two.
- Say: **If this says *breensh*, make *theensh*.** Guide the student in substituting the initial consonant blend /b/ /r/ with the consonant digraph /th/.

- Rotating around the room, have other students spell nonsense words and substitute sounds in a variety of positions.

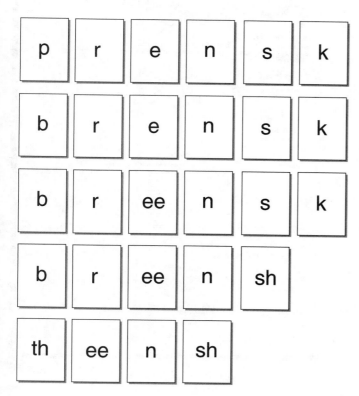

- Rotating around the room, have students shift positions in words, such as *frelk/relfk; flamst/lamfst; skloop/loopsk.*

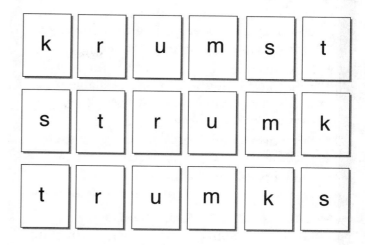

▶ DELETION ROUTINES

Explain to students that you will be deleting single consonants, consonant blends (two letters that make two sounds), or consonant digraphs (two letters that make one sound).

- Say: **If this says *gleend*, make *geend*.** Have the student remove *l* and read the new nonsense word.

- Continue this routine with other nonsense words, such as *snumd/snud; splawps/spawps; kwanst/kwant; gleend/gleen; thwomps/twomps.*

▶ SHIFTING ROUTINES

Mention to students that you will be shifting the position of letters within each word. Since this is a more challenging activity, stretch each sound as you say the nonsense word.

- Say: **If this says *krumst*, make *strumk*.** Guide a volunteer in shifting *s* and *t* to the first and second positions, and placing the *k* at the end of the word.

- Say: **If this says *strumk*, make *trumks*.** Coach the student as he or she places the *s* at the end of the word.

▶ READING ROUTINES

Blending Sounds

- After students have manipulated and spelled a variety of words, have them practice reading them.

- Write each of the words in the Word Bank on index cards. Rotating around the small group, ask each student to read a word. If students are having difficulty, say the word slowly, stretching each sound; then ask them to segment each phoneme. When they can do this successfully, have them say the word slowly, blending the sounds together. Ask them to say the sounds more quickly, forming the word.

▶ INFORMAL ASSESSMENT

- Use the Assessment Checklist found on page 70 to determine whether students are able to decode and read five- and six-sound nonsense words.

- Working in pairs, have students test each other by asking their partners to read a nonsense word they've created. In addition, students can have their partners listen as they substitute, add, or delete sounds, and then invite them to make the new word.

LESSON 1 (Part 1)

OBJECTIVES

- Students will recognize that some base words do not change when adding the suffixes *ed* or *ing*, as in *clean, cleaned, cleaning*
- Students will recognize that the final consonant is doubled in single-syllable base words that end in consonant-vowel-consonant, as in *step, stepped, stepping*
- Students will sort words according to their spelling pattern
- Students will read sentences, fill in the correct word, and identify misspelled words

WORD BANK OF REAL WORDS

pitched	jumping	swimming	splashing
running	grabbed	cleaned	tripped
cooking	shopping	talked	stopped
loaded	walking	slipping	chirping

MATERIALS

Worktext, page 46
Teacher's Manual, page 54

CHAPTER 6 LESSON 1 (Part 1)

SPELLING RULE
Some base words do not change when adding the suffixes *ed* or *ing*, as in *clean*, *cleaned*, and *cleaning*. The final consonant is doubled in single-syllable base words that end in consonant-vowel-consonant, as in *step*, *stepped*, and *stepping*.

A. Say the Words
Say each word in the Word Bank. If you have trouble reading the words, cover up *ed* or *ing* and read each base word first. Then blend the whole word together.

WORD BANK			
pitched	jumping	swimming	splashing
running	grabbed	cleaned	tripped
cooking	shopping	talked	stopped
loaded	walking	slipping	chirping

B. Sort the Words
Read the words again in the Word Bank. Sort and write each word under the correct category.

No change when adding *ed/ing*

The final consonant is doubled when adding *ed/ing*

C. Fill in the Blanks
Read the sentences and fill in the correct words. The words can be found in the Word Bank. Use each word once.

1. I _____ to go _____ in the lake.
2. Pat _____ on the phone with Jake.
3. "Let's go _____," said Maria.
4. Meg _____ her room.
5. Sam _____ on the tip of the rug.
6. Dad _____ the car with bags from the store.

46 • Chapter 6

Worktext page 46

▶ **SPELLING**

Ed and *ing*

- Explain to students that some base words don't change when adding *ed* or *ing*, as in the words *clean, cleaned, cleaning*. Mention that the final consonant is doubled in single-syllable base words that end in consonant-vowel-consonant, as in *step, stepped, stepping*. Write these words on the board and have students brainstorm other words to put in each category. Keep some dictionaries handy so that students can check their spelling.

- Have students turn to page 46 in their Worktext. Rotating around the room, ask students to read each word found in the Word Bank. Have students sort the words in the categories listed on the page.

- Ask students to "Fill in the Blanks" by finding a word in the Word Bank to complete each sentence.

LESSON 1 (Part 2)

OBJECTIVES

- Students will recognize that words with double consonants sometimes stand for one sound, such as /n/ in *dinner*
- Students will identify words containing double consonants
- Students will sort words according to the one sound each double consonant makes
- Students will read sentences, fill in the correct word, and proofread a passage

WORD BANK OF REAL WORDS

happy	slipper	ridden	hobby
bubble	written	follow	ladder
carry	balloon	berry	bottle
puppy	saddle	supper	lettuce
button	hidden	borrow	parrot

MATERIALS

Worktext, page 47
Teacher's Manual, page 55

LESSON 1 (Part 2)

SPELLING RULE
Words with double consonants sometimes stand for one sound, like /n/ in *dinner*.

A. Say the Words
Say each word in the Word Bank.

WORD BANK			
bubble	written	follow	ladder
carry	balloon	berry	rubber
puppy	saddle	supper	lettuce
button	hidden	borrow	happy

B. Sort the Words
Sort and write each word under the correct double-consonant sound category. Circle the double consonants found in each word.

/p/	/b/	/r/	/t/	/d/	/l/

C. Proofread a Note
Read the note. Find the five misspelled words and underline them. Write them correctly on the lines below.

> Dear Sal,
>
>   My pupy is very small, but cute. She likes to sit by me when I have super. I cary her when I go to the store. She likes to folow me to school. She is hapy all the time. Please stop by and meet her!
>
>   Love,
>   Deb

1. _____ 2. _____ 3. _____ 4. _____ 5. _____

Lesson 1 • 47

Worktext page 47

▶ SPELLING

Medial Double Consonants

- Write the word **dinner** on the board. Explain to students that words with double consonants sometimes stand for one sound. Say the words **slipper**, **ridden**, **hobby**, and **happy**. Have volunteers sound them out and spell them on the board.

- Have students take turns reading each of the words found in the Word Bank on Worktext page 47. Then have them sort each word according to the one sound each double consonant makes, such as /b/, /r/, /t/, /d/, and /l/.

- Have students proofread the note at the bottom of the page.

LESSON 2

OBJECTIVES

- Students will decode and read five- and six-sound words
- Students will write lists of rhyming words
- Students will build and spell words using letter cards
- Students will read clues and find words that contain five and six sounds
- Students will practice sorting three-, four-, five-, and six-sound words
- Students will play Word Search, locating five- and six-sound words

WORD BANK OF REAL WORDS

shrimp	stream	ground	float
streets	desks	skipped	lamps
plunk	splint	clasp	

MATERIALS

Worktext, pages 48–49
Teacher's Manual, pages 56–57
Award Certificate, page 71
letter cards for each pair of students

▶ RHYMING ROUTINES

- Write one of the words from the Word Bank on the board, such as **stream**. Ask students to write the word on their papers. Have them brainstorm and write down other words that have the same spelling pattern and that rhyme with it, such as **beam**, **cream**, **dream**, **gleam**, **team**. If students have difficulty spelling the words, have them practice stretching out each sound as they write.

- Invite volunteers to come up to the board and write words that you dictate from the Word Bank. Ask them to think of a rhyming word for each, such as *float/ goat/ moat/ coat/ boat*; *skipped/ dipped/ tripped*; *lamps/ stamps/ camps*; *streets/ meet/ feet*.

▶ WORD-BUILDING ROUTINES

- Provide individuals or pairs of students with a set of letter cards. Depending on what spelling pattern students need to practice, you may wish to pull specific letter cards. Or you may wish to give them a word, such as *stream*, and ask them to make as many little words as they can using only those letter cards.

- Time students in this word-building activity, then award a certificate to the individual who makes the most words in a ten-minute time period. Ask each student to read each word. The certificate is found on page 71.

▶ PRACTICE

A. Guess the Word

Have students complete the activity on page 48 in the Worktext. Students can work in pairs to read each clue and find the mystery word found in the Word Bank.

B. Sort and Search

Invite students to sort three-, four-, five-, and six-sound words found in the Word Bank.

C. Word-Search Board

Then have students locate and circle the words on the Word-Search Board.

LESSON 2

A. Guess the Word

With a partner, take turns reading each word in the Word Bank. Then read the clues below and guess which mystery word answers the clue. Use each word once.

WORD BANK		
paddle	skunk	shrimp
guppy	carrot	stream
claps	bottle	ground
flippers	street	lamps
floats	desks	skipped

Clues   **Mystery Words**

1. They need light bulbs to work. _____

2. They are found in the water and are good to eat. _____

3. We sit at them each day in school. _____

4. It is a good snack to eat. _____

5. It is black and white. _____

6. It is a small fish. _____

7. This word makes the long *o* sound. _____

8. It rhymes with *dream*. _____

9. You row with it. _____

10. You can put water in it. _____

11. It rhymes with *sound*. _____

12. The first three letters begin like *string*. _____

13. It rhymes with *taps*. _____

14. When you unscramble k-p-p-s-e-d-i, you make this word. _____

15. It rhymes with *zippers*. _____

Worktext page 48

B. Sort and Search

Congratulations! You have learned a lot about three-, four-, five-, and six-sound words. Read each word in the Word Bank. Sound out each one carefully. How many sounds does each word have? Sort the words in the correct category below. Then locate and circle each one on the Word-Search Board. Words can go down, across, diagonally, or backward. Good luck!

WORD BANK			
theme	gruff	streets	plunk
strict	spring	trick	rule
mill	clasp	lunged	wished
found	check	splint	crisp

Three-Sound Words	Four-Sound Words	Five-Sound Words	Six-Sound Words
_____	_____	_____	_____
_____	_____	_____	_____
		_____	_____
		_____	_____
		_____	

C. Word-Search Board

J	L	K	B	G	N	I	R	P	S
B	H	P	T	R	U	L	E	F	T
S	V	S	L	U	N	G	E	D	R
P	T	I	D	F	I	T	C	F	I
P	K	R	T	F	E	N	H	O	C
S	C	C	E	M	F	I	E	U	T
A	I	J	E	E	S	L	C	N	S
L	R	H	D	K	T	P	K	D	H
C	T	J	Y	W	I	S	H	E	D
J	K	N	U	L	P	M	I	L	L

Worktext page 49

LESSON 3

OBJECTIVES

- Students will apply decoding skills by reading a travel diary entry and a music review
- Students will apply their writing skills by using five- and six-sound words to write a diary entry and a music review
- Students will apply comprehension skills by answering questions about a music review

MATERIALS

Worktext, pages 50–54
Teacher's Manual, pages 58–59
Award Certificate, page 71

▶ DECODING AND READING

A. Let's Go Camping!

- Have students open to page 50 in the Worktext. Read the title "Let's Go Camping!" Mention that the word *Let's* means the same thing as *Let us*, and is called a contraction. Explain that when we talk, we often use contractions.
- Have students read aloud, taking turns reading each travel diary entry.

B. Oh, What a Trip!

Have students read the words found in the Word Bank. Ask them to pretend they've just come back from a camping trip. Brainstorm what might have happened using the words from the Word Bank. Then have students write some diary entries using these words.

C. Good Times

- Before reading the music review, write the following words on the board: **Saturday**, **people**, **guitar**, **keyboard**, **player**, and **drummer**. Ask volunteers to read the words. See if the volunteers can demonstrate on the board to the rest of the class how to decode a word if they are having difficulty, such as covering up *er* in the word *player*, and decoding *play* first. Make note of those students who have difficulty using their decoding strategies.
- Write the phrase **hot riffs** on the board. Explain that the term *riffs* means a repeated melody and that when combined with *hot* (a slang term), it means that the player executed some outstanding melodic phrases on the guitar.
- Have students read the review, coaching students if they need help decoding a challenging word.

D. Think About It

Have students read the music review and answer the questions. Remind them to answer the questions using complete sentences.

E. A Music Review

- Brainstorm music groups that students find to be their favorite and least favorite. Then have them write their own music review, describing the *who, what, where, when,* and *why* of the event.
- Give Award Certificates, found on page 71, to students who write the most creative reviews.

▶ ASSESSMENT

Dictation

Ask students to write down the following sentences as you dictate them. Be sure to say each sentence a few times before having them write. Say each sentence slowly and distinctly. If students have difficulty spelling a word, have them leave a blank or write as much of the word as they can.

1. Matt and his dad pitched the tent.
2. Pip jumped into the stream and splashed around.
3. Matt made a splint for my sprained thumb.
4. We made a fire and cooked the fish.
5. The crowd screamed, danced, and clapped to the beat.

LESSON 3

A. Let's Go Camping!
Read the travel diary entry below.

Day 1: Saturday

3:00 P.M. We got to our campsite by midday. Matt and his dad pitched the tent, while I went to the store to buy food.

4:00 P.M. When I got back from the store, my dog Pip jumped out of the truck and ran to the stream. He jumped into the stream, splashing and swimming with joy. Then Pip saw a black-and-white striped skunk! He started to run near the skunk, but I grabbed his collar to stop him. When I did, I tripped on a rock and fell. I hurt my thumb. Matt and his dad saw me fall and ran to me. We looked at my thumb and thought it might be sprained. Matt made a splint out of a small stick and tape.

5:00 P.M. While Matt and his dad went looking for wood to make a fire, I fished in the stream. Pip helped too! I caught two striped bass. Then I cleaned them so we could have a fish dinner.

6:30 P.M. When Matt and his dad got back to our camp, Matt made a fire, and we cooked the fish. I put some black beans in a pot and cooked them too. We ate the fish and dipped some bread in the beans and its sauce. Our meal was so good! As we were cleaning up, we gave Pip the food scraps. He licked his dish clean and barked for more!

8:45 P.M. When it got dark, we put our sleeping bags in the tent. We made sure there was no food in the tent. I had seen a sign at the store that said, "WATCH OUT FOR BEARS." We knew that the bears would leave us alone if we left our food in the truck, not in the tent. Then we talked and talked and started to fall asleep.

50 • Chapter 6

Worktext page 50

Day 2: Sunday

6:00 A.M. Pip and I woke up when we heard the birds chirping. Matt and his dad started to stir. We took a quick dip in the stream and ate some fruit. We took down the tent and rolled up our sleeping bags. We loaded them into the truck.

7:45 A.M. We took a three-mile hike, with Pip leading the way. While we were walking, we saw a deer running in the woods. When we got back to camp, we ate a snack and headed for home. Next month, we want to come back and camp here for three days. But next time, I do not want to sprain my thumb!

Worktext page 51

B. Oh, What a Trip!

Pretend that you and your friends just came home from a camping trip. Lots of things happened, some good and some not so good! With a partner, take turns reading the words in the Word Bank. Talk with each other about what might have happened if the two of you went on a camping trip. Write some travel diary entries about what happened, using as many of the words in the Word Bank as you can.

WORD BANK			
scratched	tents	splashing	swimming
skunks	tripped	bears	screamed
drenched	shivered	cooked	camping
jumped	stream	fished	running
slipped	sprained	grabbed	pitched

My Diary

Day 1: _____

_____

_____

_____

Day 2: _____

_____

_____

_____

Day 3: _____

_____

_____

_____

Day 4: _____

_____

_____

_____

Day 5: _____

_____

_____

_____

Worktext page 52

C. Good Times
Read the following article.

Rock 'n' Roll in the Park

Last Saturday, the Good Time Rockers, a group from Los Angeles, played to a crowd of more than 1,000 people at Stone Park. The crowd sat on the ground and ate food as the group played old rock tunes from the 1950s and 1960s. The crowd screamed and sang along. Some people got up and danced as they snapped and clapped to the beat. The guitar player made up some hot riffs on a slow song. When it ended, the crowd shouted for more. Then the keyboard player started a new tune, with the bass player singing lead. On one song, the drummer played a 20-minute solo and had the crowd cheering. All in all, the Good Time Rockers is the best rock group that has ever played at Stone Park.

Worktext page 53

D. Think About It

Reread "Rock 'n' Roll in the Park." Then answer the questions below.

1. On what day did the Good Time Rockers perform? _____
2. Where does this music group live? _____
3. What kind of music does it play? _____
4. How many players are in the group? _____
5. What instruments do they play? _____

   _____
6. How did the crowd react to the music? _____

   _____
7. Who played a solo? _____
8. What did the music reviewer think of the group? _____

E. A Music Review

Write your own music review about your favorite or least favorite music group. Be sure to include the following:

- *Who* performed?
- *What* kind of music did the group sing or play?
- *Where* did it perform?
- *When* did it perform?
- *Why* did you like the group? Why didn't you like the group?

_____

_____

_____

_____

_____

_____

_____

_____

_____

_____

Worktext page 54

CHAPTER 7
Two-Syllable, Compound, and Multisyllabic Words

LESSON 1

OBJECTIVES
- Students will develop phonemic awareness as they identify words containing more than one syllable
- Students will connect sounds to letters by identifying the number of vowel sounds in two-syllable words
- Students will decode, read, and spell words containing two syllables

WORD BANK OF TWO-SYLLABLE WORDS

visit	almost	pencil	lemon
barrel	chicken	orchard	respect
welcome	zebra	doctor	either
feather	gallon	machine	quarter
travel	unite	harbor	invite
jelly	kitten	never	shoulder

MATERIALS
Worktext, page 55
Teacher's Manual, page 60
letter cards

▶ PHONEMIC AWARENESS
Clapping Syllable Patterns

- Introduce the concept that words can have more than one syllable by asking students to repeat each of the following words after you: **money, imagination, grocery, invitation, encyclopedia**. Ask them to say the words again, this time clapping the rhythm or counting the syllables on their fingers. Have volunteers say the number of syllables in each word.

- Invite students to think of big words to share with classmates, and have them clap and count the syllables.

▶ PHONICS
Connecting Sounds to Letters

- Mention that a lot of words are made up of syllables, or smaller parts. Write **gallon** on the board. Recall that in Chapter 6, students learned about words that contain double consonants, such as the /l/ in *gallon*. Point out that this word contains a vowel in each syllable, the /a/ and /o/. Write **welcome** on the board and invite a student

to come up to the board and circle each vowel. Then ask the student to decode each syllable and blend the sounds together to form the word.

- Have students brainstorm other two-syllable words, inviting them to sound out and spell the words on the board.

▶ WORD-BUILDING ROUTINES

Using letter cards, ask students to build the word *lemon*. Students can work independently or in pairs for this activity. After they've spelled words successfully, have them think of two-syllable words for the class to spell. Using a checklist, record the types of errors students make, identifying whether they're making mistakes with vowel sounds, or initial, medial, or final consonants.

▶ PRACTICE

- Have students turn to page 55 in the Worktext and take turns reading the words in the Word Bank. Then ask them to circle the vowels contained in the first and second syllable of each word.

- Ask students to read the sentences and fill in the missing words. Each word can be found in the Word Bank.

- Students then read and underline each two-syllable word in the passage.

CHAPTER 7 LESSON 1

A. Say the Words
Working with a partner, take turns reading each word in the Word Bank. Then circle the two vowels found in the first and second syllable of each word.

WORD BANK

visit	almost	pencil	lemon
barrel	chicken	orchard	respect
welcome	zebra	doctor	either
feather	gallon	machine	quarter
travel	unite	harbor	invite
jelly	kitten	never	shoulder

B. Fill in the Blanks
Read each sentence and fill in the missing word. Use your Word Bank for help. Use each word once.

1. "_____ home," said Joe to his Uncle Jeff.
2. I have a _____ tree in my front yard.
3. Jenny wanted to _____ a friend to her house after school.
4. Let's have _____ for dinner.
5. I need a _____ to write my paper.
6. Marge went to the store to buy a _____ jug of milk.
7. Nick's _____ ran into the apple _____.
8. We like to _____ by either plane or train.
9. I paid a _____ for a small pack of gum.
10. On Saturday, I'm going to _____ my friend Sam.

C. Read and Underline
Read the following passage and underline all the two-syllable words. Some of these words will not be found in the Word Bank. Good luck!

On Sunday, Mark will invite his friends Peg and Steven to supper. He will serve lemon chicken, rice, and soda. After supper, they will go into the apple orchard and pick apples, filling up an entire barrel. When it gets dark, they will go inside and make gallons of apple cider and seven apple pies.

Lesson 1 • 55

Worktext page 55

LESSON 2

OBJECTIVES

- Students will develop phonemic awareness as they identify the similarities in compound words
- Students will connect sounds to letters by recognizing that compound words are made up of smaller words
- Students will decode, read, and spell compound words

WORD BANK OF COMPOUND WORDS

basketball	baseball	football	birthday
outhouse	lighthouse	inside	softball
beside	sunflower	snowball	today
carport	raincoat	sunshine	
snowflake	airport	raindrop	
seaport	snowplow	Sunday	
fireball	sunlight	rainbow	
sunset	snowsuit	outside	

MATERIALS

Worktext, page 56
Teacher's Manual, page 61

▶ PHONEMIC AWARENESS

Compound Words

- Ask students what the following words have in common: **basketball**, **baseball**, **football**. If students say that they are all types of sports, praise them. Then ask them if the words sound similar in any way. Students should say that they all end in *ball*.

- Say another set of words, such as **outhouse** and **lighthouse**. Ask students to determine the similarities in these words.

▶ PHONICS

Connecting Sounds to Letters

- Mention that all of these are compound words, which are made up of smaller words. Using paper and pencils, have students write the words **basketball**, **baseball**, and **football**. If they have difficulty, have them write the similar part in each word first, then add on the parts that are different. Do the same routine with *outhouse, lighthouse, inside, outside,* and *beside.*

▶ PRACTICE

- Have students turn to page 56 in their Worktexts and take turns reading the compound words found in the Word Bank.

- Ask them to sort the words according to similar smaller words contained in each compound word.

- Invite students to match up small words to make compound words.

- Have students read the sentences and underline the compound words that don't make sense. Ask them to write the correct word in the space provided.

LESSON 2

A. Say and Sort the Words

Read the compound words found in the Word Bank. Then sort each word according to similar smaller words contained in each compound word. Two words are used twice.

WORD BANK			
sunflower	snowball	birthday	carport
raincoat	sunshine	softball	snowflake
airport	raindrop	today	seaport
snowplow	Sunday	fireball	sunlight
rainbow	snowsuit		

sun-	snow-	rain-	-ball	-port	-day

B. Make a Bigger Word

Look at the words in each box. Combine a word in the first box with a word in the second box to make a bigger word. Write each compound word below.

| butter |
| good |
| rattle |
| under |

| snake |
| fly |
| stand |
| bye |

1. _____ 2. _____ 3. _____ 4. _____

C. Make Sense!

Read each sentence. Find and underline the compound word that does not make sense. Write the correct word after each sentence. Use the Word Bank for help.

1. The child wore a snowsuit when it rained. _____
2. The raindrop bloomed in spring. _____
3. I pitched a snowball to the player who was batting for the home team. _____
4. I parked my boat in the carport. _____

56 • Chapter 7

Worktext page 56

LESSON 3

OBJECTIVES

- Students will develop phonemic awareness as they identify words containing prefixes
- Students will decode by analogy as they identify similar word parts or chunks
- Students will decode, read, and spell words containing prefixes

WORD BANK OF WORDS CONTAINING PREFIXES

exchange	export	exhale	express
depart	deport	deplane	decrease
disappoint	disapprove	disagree	disinterest
unfair	unlike	unpack	unwrap
unhappy	untie	unfold	unlucky
reread	rework	return	replace
refill	rebuild	rewrite	rebound

MATERIALS

Worktext, page 57
Teacher's Manual, page 62

▶ PHONEMIC AWARENESS

Similar Word Parts

- Say the following words to students: **exchange**, **export**, **exhale**, **express**. Ask them to decide what feature is similar among the words. When students say that the words begin the same way, repeat each word and invite them to echo you. Do the same routine with other words in the Word Bank.
- Say the following words to students: **disagree**, **disinterest**, **depart**, **disapprove**. Ask them to name the word that isn't the same. Do this routine with other words.

▶ PHONICS

Decoding by Analogy

- Write the words **exchange**, **export**, **exhale**, and **express** on the board. Have a volunteer circle the word part that is similar in each word and underline the word parts that are different. Explain that *ex* is a prefix or word chunk that is added at the beginning of a base word. Mention that prefixes change the meaning of the word. In this case, *ex* means *out of* or *from*.
- Do this routine with other words found in the Word Bank.

- You may want to mention that *un* usually means *not*; *dis* usually means *the opposite of*; *re* usually means *do again* or *back*; *de* usually means *go away from* or *step down*.

▶ PRACTICE

- Have students turn to page 57 in the Worktext. Rotating around the room, have students read the words in the Word Bank. Ask them to circle each prefix and underline the base words.
- Ask students to complete the sentences by filling in the blanks with words found in the Word Bank.
- Have students proofread the passage and write the correct spellings for each word.

LESSON 3

A. Say the Words
Read the words found in the Word Bank. Then circle each prefix and underline the base words. Remember that the prefix is the word part or chunk found at the beginning of each word.

WORD BANK			
exchange	deport	disinterest	rebuild
unfair	reread	unlike	disapprove
exhale	deplane	rewrite	unhappy
disappoint	depart	express	unwrap
rebound	untie	refill	unpack
export	unlucky	replace	rework
unfold	return	disagree	decrease

B. Fill in the Blanks
Read each sentence and fill in the missing word. Use your Word Bank for help.

1. I think that it is _____ that we only have 20 minutes to eat lunch.
2. Pat was very _____ with her spelling grade.
3. Jay _____ the poem before he wrote his own.
4. I _____ with the law that was just put into effect.
5. Sally and Rob are going to _____ the car's engine.

C. Proofread It
Read the following paragraph and circle the five words that are misspelled. Write the correct spellings below.

> I was unhapy when I came home from my trip because I had such a good time. The first thing I did was to unpak my suitcase. Then I wrote my friend a note to expres to her how much fun I had. I told her that I would like to retirn to her town for a visit during spring break. I rered my note before sending it to her.

1. _____ 2. _____ 3. _____ 4. _____ 5. _____

Lesson 3 • 57

Worktext page 57

LESSON 4

OBJECTIVES
- Students will develop phonemic awareness as they identify words containing suffixes
- Students will decode by analogy as they identify similar word parts or chunks
- Students will decode, read, and spell words containing suffixes

WORD BANK OF WORDS CONTAINING SUFFIXES

careful	thankful	painful	helpful
hopeful	harmful	useful	thoughtful
careless	thankless	painless	helpless
hopeless	harmless	useless	thoughtless
washable	dependable	breakable	reliable
sinkable	honorable		

MATERIALS
Worktext, page 58
Teacher's Manual, page 63

▶ PHONEMIC AWARENESS

Suffixes
- Say the words **washable**, **breakable**, and **sinkable**. Ask students to name the word chunk that is similar in each word. (*able*) Explain to students that *able* means *able to* or *full of*. Tell them that a suffix is a word part that is attached at the end of a base word.
- Do this routine with other words found in the Word Bank. Explain that *ful* means *full of*; *less* means *without*.

▶ PHONICS

Decoding by Analogy
- Write **careful** on the board. Ask students to think of other words that they know that end in *ful*, such as *useful, thoughtful, hopeful,* and *painful.* Have them write these words as students brainstorm each.
- Have students spell other words found in the Word Bank by asking them to think of other words that have similar word chunks.

▶ PRACTICE
- Ask students to turn to page 58 in the Worktext. Have them take turns reading each of the words. Afterward, they can circle the suffixes and underline each base word.
- Have students reread the words in the Word Bank and sort them according to their endings.
- Ask students to complete the sentences by filling in the appropriate words.

LESSON 4

A. Say the Words
Read each word found in the Word Bank. Then circle the suffixes and underline the base words. Remember that suffixes are the word parts or chunks found at the end of words.

WORD BANK			
careful	harmless	washable	reliable
helpless	thankful	hopeless	helpful
honorable	painless	thoughtful	breakable
sinkable	thankless	useless	thoughtless
hopeful	careless	painful	useful
dependable	harmful		

B. Sort the Words
Reread each word and sort them according to their endings.

-ful	-less	-able
_____	_____	_____
_____	_____	_____
_____	_____	_____
_____	_____	_____
_____	_____	
_____	_____	
_____		

C. Fill in the Blanks
Read each sentence and fill in the missing word. Use the Word Bank if you need help. More than one word may complete some of the sentences.

1. I felt very _____ when I could help Mom set the table.
2. I have to be careful because the dishes are _____.
3. Randy was _____ when the car did not hit him.
4. She is a very _____ sister.
5. I am very _____ when I hold my baby brother.

58 • Chapter 7

Worktext page 58

LESSON 5

OBJECTIVES
- Students will apply their decoding skills by reading poems that contain compound, two-syllable, and multisyllabic words
- Students will apply their writing skills by writing a poem and a paragraph about themselves

MATERIALS
Worktext, page 59–62
Teacher's Manual, pages 64–65
Award Certificate, page 71

▶ DECODING AND READING

A. Compound Raps

Have students turn to page 59 in their Worktexts. Mention that "Seasons" and "What's the Score?" are two poems or raps that have a steady, toe-tapping, finger-snapping rhythm. Explain that each of them contains compound words. Ask students to scan the text silently to see if there are words they have difficulty decoding. Write them on the board and have volunteers help the class to read them, demonstrating their decoding strategies. Then have students read the text.

B. Find the Compound Words

Invite students to reread "Seasons." Then ask them to underline all of the compound words. Afterward, have them draw a line in between the two smaller words that make up each compound word. Encourage them to check their answers using a dictionary.

C. Write Your Own Rap or Poem

Ask students to write their own poem or rap using some of the words found in the Word Bank. Students can also brainstorm some compound words of their own or use some that are found in the two raps they just read.

D. Beginnings and Endings
I Am Able

- Review prefixes and suffixes with students; then have them scan the text for words that may be difficult to decode. Write the words on the board and guide students as they employ their decoding strategies. First, have them look at the base word and decode it. Then move to the prefix or suffix.

- If a word has both a prefix and suffix, decode the suffix first; then move to the prefix. When students are able to decode all of the word parts or chunks, then ask them to blend the parts together to form the word. Finally, have students read the poem, "I Am Able."

E. Count the Syllables

Ask students to reread the poem. Have pairs of students look for words that contain more than one syllable. Have them draw lines in between each syllable; then have them check their answers using a dictionary.

F. Sorting for Syllables

Invite students to read the poem again. Have them find and sort four words for each category, according to how many syllables the words contain.

G. I Am _____

With lots of enthusiasm, tell your students "Congratulations—for a job well done!" Mention that they have just completed *Getting Ready* and have the skills necessary to move forward into *Caught Reading Plus*. As a celebration, award each student a certificate, found on page 71. Then ask them to write a short paragraph about themselves, describing all the positive qualities that they possess. Brainstorm a list of words and have them spell and write each one on the board. Ask students to think of one word that sums them up, and to use it in the title.

▶ ASSESSMENT

Dictation

As a final dictation activity, use some of the sentences that students wrote to describe themselves, such as *I am a person worthy of love. I am helpful and reliable in class. I am thoughtful to my family and friends. I am interested in listening to what my brother has to say. I am cheerful and happy—and it rubs off onto others!*

Worktext page 59

A. Compound Raps
Read the following poems.

Seasons

Winter, spring, summer, and fall.
Tell me the season that's best of all.
Raincoats, raindrops, rainbows too.
Spring has rain showers that rain on you!
Spring turns to summer. Did you know?
Buttercups bloom and sunflowers grow.
Summertime is fun at the sunny seashore.
Let's find seashells. Time to explore!
Fall is the time for a football game.
Cheerleaders cheer each player's name.
Wintertime is cold with lots of snowflakes,
Snowballs, snowsuits, and icy lakes.

What's the Score?

Baseball and basketball can be fun.
Football is the sport where you run, run, run!
Fullback, quarterback, linebacker too.
Root for the team in red and blue.
Watch the scoreboard. What's the score?
Make a touchdown. We want more!

Lesson 5 • 59

Worktext page 60

B. Find the Compound Words
Reread the rap below. Find each compound word and underline it.
Then draw a line in between the two smaller words that make up
each compound word.

Seasons

Winter, spring, summer, and fall.
Tell me the season that's best of all.
Raincoats, raindrops, rainbows too.
Spring has rain showers that rain on you!
Spring turns to summer. Did you know?
Buttercups bloom and sunflowers grow.
Summertime is fun at the sunny seashore.
Let's find seashells. Time to explore!
Fall is the time for a football game.
Cheerleaders cheer each player's name.
Wintertime is cold with lots of snowflakes,
Snowballs, snowsuits, and icy lakes.

C. Write Your Own Rap or Poem
Write your own rap or poem using some of the words in the Word
Bank. You can use a dictionary or brainstorm other words that you
would like to use.

WORD BANK		
newspaper	goldfish	sweatshirt
breakfast	grapefruit	strawberry
doorbell	seashell	flashlight
something	anywhere	volleyball
inside	outside	weekend
sailboat	sunset	football

_____
_____
_____
_____
_____
_____

60 • Chapter 7

Worktext page 61

D. Beginnings and Endings
Read the following poem.

I Am Able

Un can begin some words you see.
Unbeatable and unafraid can describe me.
Inactive and intolerant are just not "in."
Be involved and interested. You'll fit right in!
Able can end some words for you,
Like reliable, dependable, and honorable too.
Thankful and bashful are sometimes me.
Thoughtful and helpful are always me!
Foolish and childish, I am not.
Admirable qualities are what I've got!

Lesson 5 • 61

Worktext page 62

E. Count the Syllables
Reread "I Am Able." Then look for words that contain more than one
syllable. Draw a line between each syllable. Check your answers by
looking up the words in the dictionary.

I Am Able

Un can begin some words you see.
Unbeatable and unafraid can describe me.
Inactive and intolerant are just not "in."
Be involved and interested. You'll fit right in!
Able can end some words for you,
Like reliable, dependable, and honorable too.
Thankful and bashful are sometimes me.
Thoughtful and helpful are always me!
Foolish and childish, I am not.
Admirable qualities are what I've got!

F. Sorting for Syllables
As you read the poem again, find and sort four words for each
category, according to how many syllables the words contain.

One syllable	Two syllables	Three syllables	Four syllables
_____	_____	_____	_____
_____	_____	_____	_____
_____	_____	_____	_____
_____	_____	_____	_____

G. I Am _____
Write a paragraph that describes what you are like as a person. Think
about all of the positive qualities that you have. Then choose one
word that sums you up and use it in the title of this activity.

Title: _____

_____
_____
_____
_____
_____

62 • Chapter 7

FINAL ASSESSMENT

Introducing the Test

The Final Assessment on pages 67-69 is designed to help you measure your students' mastery of basic reading skills. Based on their scores, you will either:
- move students into *Caught Reading Plus*, Level 1 or
- review concepts from the *Getting Ready* program

Administering the Test

The test is designed to be administered in a single session. Distribute copies of the test to your students. In order to measure fluency, you may wish to have your students read the items from exercises E and G aloud.

Scoring the Test

There are 72 items on the test. Your students should score 80% or better (or 57 correct answers) to be moved into *Caught Reading Plus*, Level 1. Students who score less than 80% need to review *Getting Ready*.

Remember that 80% is a general guideline. Use your firsthand knowledge of your students in conjunction with their test scores to ensure proper placement. For instance, if you have a student that scores 83%, but you have seen him/her struggling throughout your instruction of the material, review the key concepts in the *Getting Ready Teacher's Manual* one more time before moving him/her to *Caught Reading Plus*, Level 1.

Final Assessment Answer Key

Exercise A
1. chop
2. kick
3. bad/dab
4. pen
5. fill
6. pass
7. cuff
8. meat/team
9. coin
10. wheel
11. boat
12. farm
13. blue
14. true
15. aunt
16. grew
17. three
18. den
19. play
20. tree

Exercise B
1. pan/pen/pin/pun
2. mad/man/map/mar/mat/may
3. but/cut/gut/hut/jut/nut/rut
4. fan/fin/fun
5. tab/tag/tan/tap/tar/tat
6. bug/dug/jug/lug/mug/rug/tug
7. hat/hit/hot/hut
8. tap/tip/top
9. bid/did/hid/kid/lid/rid/
10. pad/pal/pan/sad/tad/wad

Exercise C
1. pay/lay
2. hid
3. cub
4. fee
5. bank
6. cap/lap
7. fog
8. mat/ate
9. cat/cot
10. ant

Exercise D

Short-vowel words	Long-vowel words
catch	peach
mud	mate
sled	drove
frog	cute
chip	write
send	wheel

Exercise E
1. hike, trail
2. climb
3. brown
4. swimming
5. tripped
6. saddle
7. stream
8. struts

Exercise F
1. softball
2. snowflake
3. rainbow
4. today
5. sunlight
6. airport

Exercise G
1. unfasten
2. refill
3. hopeful, sunny
4. careful
5. washable
6. dislike

FINAL ASSESSMENT

A. Unscramble the Words

Below is a series of words to unscramble. When you unscramble
the word, write it. Then read the word and place a check mark next
to the word, indicating that you read it.

	Example			Write it.	Read it.
	t	a	th	*that*	☑
1.	ch	p	o	_____	❑
2.	i	ck	k	_____	❑
3.	d	b	a	_____	❑
4.	n	p	e	_____	❑
5.	f	ll	i	_____	❑
6.	a	p	ss	_____	❑
7.	u	ff	c	_____	❑
8.	ea	m	t	_____	❑
9.	n	oi	c	_____	❑
10.	ee	wh	l	_____	❑
11.	b	t	oa	_____	❑
12.	ar	m	f	_____	❑
13.	l	ue	b	_____	❑
14.	r	t	ue	_____	❑
15.	n	au	t	_____	❑
16.	g	ew	r	_____	❑
17.	th	ee	r	_____	❑
18.	n	d	e	_____	❑
19.	ay	l	p	_____	❑
20.	ee	r	t	_____	❑

B. Substitute Sounds and Letters

Look at each word and fill in the blank to make a word. If you can think of other words to make using other letters, write these words, too.

Example: c ___ p   _cap, cop, cup_

1. p __ n   _____
2. m a __   _____
3. ___ u t   _____
4. f ___ n   _____
5. t a ___   _____

6. ___ u g   _____
7. h ___ t   _____
8. t ___ p   _____
9. ___ i d   _____
10. p a ___   _____

C. Delete Sounds and Letters

Look at each word. Delete one letter to make a new word.

Example: **plan**   _____pan_____

   plane   _____plan_____

1. play   _____
2. hide   _____
3. cube   _____
4. free   _____
5. blank   _____

6. clap   _____
7. frog   _____
8. mate   _____
9. coat   _____
10. aunt   _____

D. Sort the Words

Read each word in the Word Bank. Sort and write each word under the correct category.

WORD BANK			
peach	cute	write	chip
mate	catch	sled	wheel
drove	mud	frog	send

Short-vowel words

_____

_____

_____

_____

_____

_____

Long-vowel words

_____

_____

_____

_____

_____

_____

E. Fill in the Blanks

Read each sentence and fill in the correct word. The words can be found in the Word Bank. Use each word once.

WORD BANK		
climb	brown	swimming
saddle	streets	hike
trail	stream	tripped

1. When you _____, follow the _____.
2. Be careful when you _____.
3. I see a _____ bear in the woods.
4. Pam likes to go _____ in the pond.
5. Jeff _____ over a large dog.
6. I will put a _____ on the horse.
7. The puppy drank from the _____.
8. The _____ are wet from the rain.

F. Make a Bigger Word

Look at the words in each box. Combine a word in one box with a word in the other box to make a bigger word. Write each compound word below.

soft	port
snow	light
rain	bow
to	flake
sun	day
air	ball

1. _____   4. _____
2. _____   5. _____
3. _____   6. _____

G. Is It a Prefix or Suffix?

Read each sentence. Underline the words that contain a prefix. Circle the words that contain a suffix. Remember, a prefix is a word part, or chunk, found at the beginning of a word. A suffix is a word part, or chunk, found at the end of a word.

1. Please do not unfasten your seat belt.
2. I would like to refill my drink.
3. José is hopeful that it will be a sunny day.
4. We are careful when we ski down the slope.
5. My shirt is washable.
6. Sam and Sally dislike snakes.

ASSESSMENT CHECKLIST

Place letter cards on the table. Say each word slowly. Have students take turns saying and spelling each word. Record student performance here for your records.

	Student name	Nonsense or real word	Score	Notes
1.				
2.				
3.				
4.				
5.				
6.				
7.				
8.				
9.				
10.				
11.				
12.				
13.				
14.				
15.				
16.				
17.				
18.				
19.				
20.				
21.				
22.				
23.				
24.				
25.				
26.				
27.				
28.				
29.				
30.				

Score: _____

CERTIFICATE OF ACHIEVEMENT

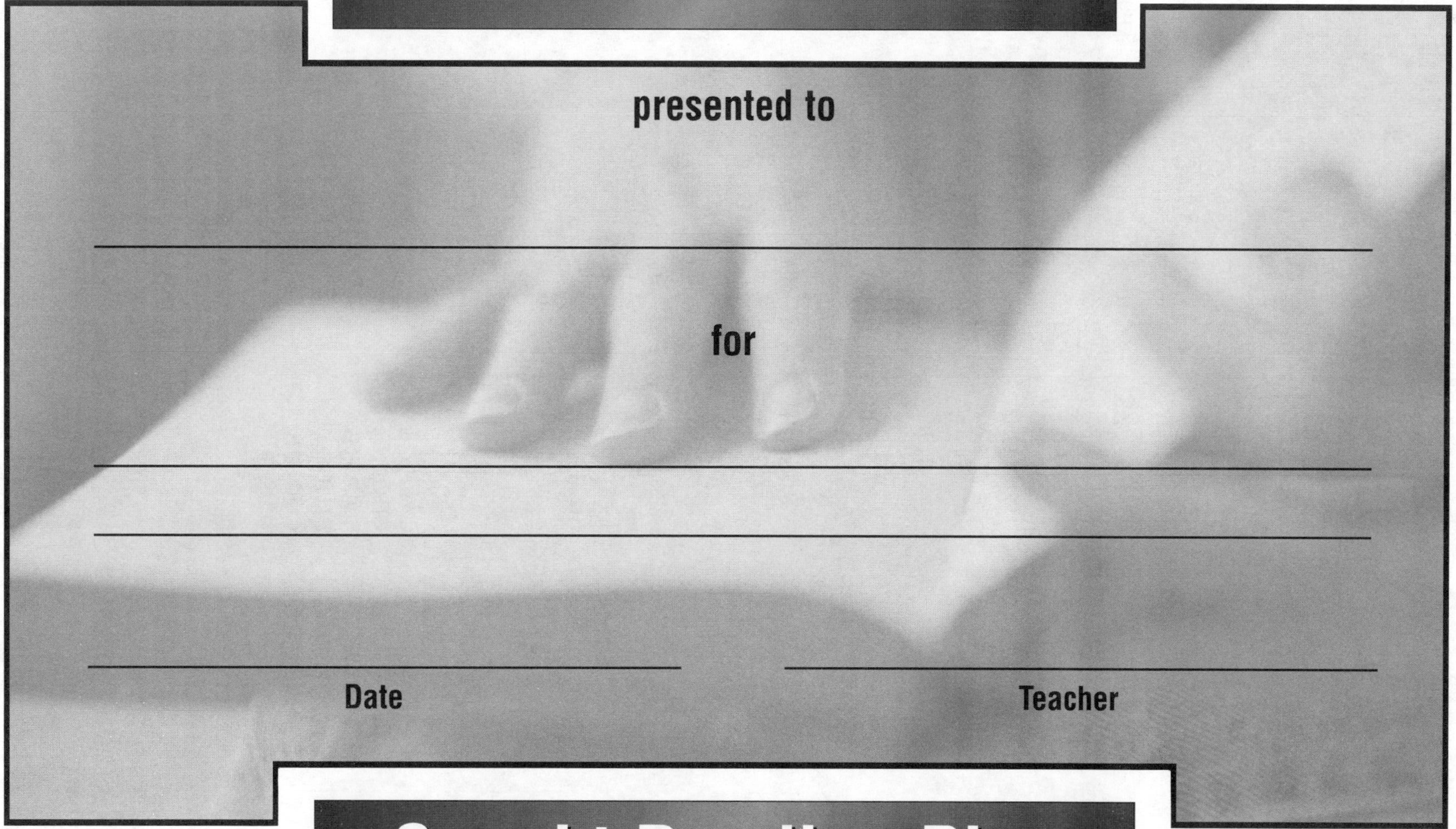

presented to

_____

for

_____

_____

_____

Teacher _____

Date _____

Caught Reading Plus

ADDITIONAL NONSENSE WORDS

Chapter 2

TIJ	MOZ	GAM	TUS	RAJ
KIJ	BOZ	GAD	TIS	REJ
LIJ	VOZ	GAV	TES	RUJ
MIJ	ROZ	GAF	TAS	RIJ
DIJ	TOZ	GAZ	TOS	ROJ
RIJ	VOZ	GAN		
PIJ	THOZ	GAJ		
VIJ		GAT		
SIJ		GAK		
WIJ		GAG		

Chapter 3

ZOOK	FAISH	MEEP	DOOP	LEEZ	SOOF	TOOT	TAISH	KOUF
ZOIK	FAIM	MAIP	DOOJ	LAIZ		TAIT	TOUSH	SHOUF
ZEEK	FAID	MOOP	DOOZ	LOOZ			TEESH	ROUF
ZIEK	FAIP	MAUP	DOOV	LOIZ			TOISH	DOUF
ZAIK	FAIZ	MOIP	DOOG	LOAZ			TOOSH	GOUF
		MOUP		LAWZ			TAUSH	LAIF
		MOAP		LOUZ				LAICH
		JOWP		TEEB				MAICH
		JOOP		IEEB				MAIZ
		JOAK		NEEB				MOIZ
				SEEB				
				CHEEB				
				SOUK				
				SOUF				

Chapter 4

ETS	SKOI	PROA	GLI	SNOU
EST	KOIS	ROAP	LIG	SOUN
TES	OISK	OARP	ILG	OUNS
STE	OIKS	POAR	GIL	NOUS

Chapter 5

STROI	ULFS	SPLEE	CHOUST
TROIS	LUFS	PLEES	SOUCHT
ROIST	SLUF	SPEEL	STOUCH
ROITS	SULT		CHOUTS

Chapter 6

SPROFT	SLOAKT	ROIMPT	TRAIKS
PROFTS	SKLOAT	PROIMT	STRAIK
PROFST	SKOALT	TROIMP	SKARAIT
SPROT	STOALK	TOIMP	SKAIRT
	SKOALT	TOIP	KAIRTS
		TOISP	KAIRST

Chapter 1

LESSON 1 a, e, i, o, and u should be circled; b, c, d, f, g, h, j, k, l, m, n, p, q, r, s, t, v, w, x, y, and z should have a square around it.

LESSON 2

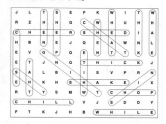

LESSON 3 1. game 2. need 3. bike 4. cove 5. tune 6. main 7. deep 8. tie 9. row 10. mule 11. day 12. meal 13. kite 14. boat 15. June 16. rain 17. each 18. pie 19. soap 20. cute

LESSON 4 A. *short a*: an, tap, at, am; *short e*: Ed, hen, get, beg; *short i*: it, if, in, sip; *short o*: mop, cot, on, log; *short u*: us, tub, bug, up; B. 1. pan, pen, pin, pun 2. tag, tug 3. mat, met 4. bat, bet, bit, but 5. fan, fin, fun 6. nod 7. ran, run 8. sap, sip, sop, sup 9. van 10. tab, tub

LESSON 5 A. *ou*: cloud, mouth, house; *ow*: bow, flower, crown; *oi*: coin, noise, oil; *oy*: boy, toy, joy; *au*: Paul, haul, pause; *aw*: crawl, yawn, paw; B. 1. coin 2. crawl 3. noise 4. mouth 5. flower 6. pause 7. cloud 8. crown 9. haul 10. yawn

Chapter 2

LESSON 1 B. *ll*: hill, fell, full, will, well; *ss*: pass, boss, miss, mess, less; *ff*: buff, stuff, cliff, puff, cuff; *ck*: back, pack, pick, kick, duck; C. 1. boss 2. chill 3. black 4. moss 5. less 6. fell 7. shack 8. pall, pass, pack 9. cuff 10. hill, hiss; D. Answers will vary.

LESSON 2 1. chat 2. cuff 3. tub or but 4. sit 5. met 6. chin 7. gab or bag 8. shop or posh 9. back 10. job 11. pick 12. lip 13. nap or pan 14. fog 15. chum or much 16. will 17. pet 18. shop or posh 19. sad 20. duck

B.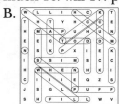

LESSON 3 B. *short a*: Pal, and, Pat, Pam; *short e*: Peg, pet, pen; *short i*: pickle, pig, pit; *short o*: pot, of, Pod, on; *short u*: put, Pug; Answers to the second part will vary. C. Answers will vary. E. 1. Red is washed. Red is fed. Red is petted. Red and his owner sit on the bed. 2. Red gets sick. Red and his owner go to the vet. Red licks the vet's chin. The vet

gets all wet. 3. Red and his owner go to the shop. They buy a pot. They buy a pan. They buy a mop. 4. Red's owner puts the pot in her van. She puts the mop in her van. She puts the pan in her van. She puts Red in her van. 5. Red and his owner go home. Red sits in his owner's lap. Red is petted. Red and his owner take a nap.

Chapter 3

LESSON 1, PART 1 B. *a-consonant-e*: fate, cane, pane, tape, made; *i-consonant-e*: hide, kite, dime, ride, bite; *o-consonant-e*: note, mope, robe, cope, hope; *u-consonant-e*: cube, cure, tube, dude, cute; C. 1. cute 2. mope 3. tape 4. note 5. bite 6. dude 7. dime 8. kite 9. fate 10. ride; D. Answers will vary.

PART 2 B. *ee*: beet, peek, feet, cheep, meet; *ea*: peak, cheap, meat, feat, beat; *ai*: gain, nail, maid, paid; *ay*: way, may, day, hay, pay; *oa*: soap, coat, foam, boat, goal; C. 1. meet or meat 2. foam 3. feet or feat 4. peek or peak 5. day 6. coat 7. beat, beet, or boat 8. nail; D. (Order of the answers may vary.) 1. cheep and cheap 2. meet and meat 3. feat and feet 4. peek and peak

LESSON 2 B. Answers will vary.

LESSON 3 B. *a-consonant-e*: Kate, made, shape, game, race, Gabe, take, lake, save, date, Nate's, wake; *i-consonant-e*: time, hike, ride, bike, dive, while, five, nine, miles, Mike; *o-consonant-e*: Hope, note; *ea*: team, seat; *ee*: need, week, sleep; *oa*: boat; C. (Answers must appear in this order, except for Gabe and Hope.) week, game, team, Gabe, Hope, need, take, beach, feed, wait, may; E. Answers will vary.

Chapter 4

LESSON 1, PART 1 B. /*s*/: city, race, mice, dice, rice, face, ice; /*k*/ coal, cat, cake, coin, cut, cone, coat; C. 1. cat, mice 2. race 3. face 4. ice 5. coat 6. ice; cone

PART 2 B. /*g*/: game, goat, egg, gum, gift; /*j*/: sage, huge, gym, page, siege; C. 1. egg 2. game 3. gum 4. gift 5. page 6. gym

PART 3 B. /*i*/: fly, my, sky, cry, by, try; /*e*/: baby, funny, very, many, puppy, pretty; C. 1. underline puppy; circle shy, my 2. underline baby; circle cry 3. circle sky 4. underline funny 5. underline many, very, and funny; circle my 6. circle fly

LESSON 2

B.

C. 1. grew 2. arch or char 3. stay 4. clue 5. aunt
6. cat or act 7. seat or eats 8. true 9. free or reef
10. glue 11. plow 12. try 13. glow 14. stew 15. rat, tar
or art 16. growl 17. math 18. three 19. oats 20. arm,
ram, or mar

LESSON 3 B. 1. Cody, Jane, Ned, and Kate
2. organizing the food drive 3. Friday 4. Room 101
5. to help the homeless people in the city;
D. 1. broke 2. arm 3. track 4. last 5. help 6. cast;
E. Answers will vary. F. Answers will vary.

Chapter 5

LESSON 1, PART 1 B. *kn*: knit, kneel, knob,
know, knife; *wr*: wreck, wren, write, wrist, wrench; *gn*:
design, sign, gnaw; *mb*: limb, comb, climb, lamb,
thumb; Students should have circled the k's, w's, g's,
and b's. C. wrist, thumb, knit, lamb, write.

PART 2 C. *ar*: car, march, large, hard; *or*: corn,
shore, sport, form, storm; *er*: nerve, verb, serve, germ;
ir: girl, first, thirst, skirt; *ur*: hurt, church, turn;
C. 1. circle car and storm 2. circle First and shore
3. circle corn and large 4. circle skirt 5. circle turn
6. circle form 7. circle nerve 8. circle church

PART 3 B. *ch*: which, reach, march; *tch*: watch,
pitch, catch; *ng*: wrong, long, sing; *nk*: pink, think,
drink; C. 1. pitch 2. Which 3. catch 4. pink or long;
D. 1. sing or sink 2. pitch 3. march 4. wrong
5. drink 6. which 7. think or thing 8. ring or rink

LESSON 2
A.

LESSON 3 C. circle front, school, form, next,
curb, turn, right, left, Trail, train, tracks; D. Answers
will vary. E. Answers will vary. G. Answers will vary.

Chapter 6

LESSON 1, PART 1 B. *No change*: pitched, cook-
ing, loaded, jumping, walking, cleaned, talked,
splashing, chirping; *doubled consonant*: running,
grabbed, shopping, swimming, slipping, tripped,
stopped; C. 1. stopped, swimming 2. talked 3. shopping 4. cleaned 5. tripped 6. loaded

PART 2 B. /p/: puppy, supper, happy; /b/: bubble,
rubber; /r/: carry, berry, borrow; /t/: button, written,
lettuce; /d/: saddle, hidden, ladder; /l/: balloon, follow; C. puppy, supper, carry, follow, happy

LESSON 2 A. 1. lamps 2. shrimp 3. desks
4. carrot 5. skunk 6. guppy 7. floats 8. stream
9. paddle 10. bottle 11. ground 12. street 13. claps
14. skipped 15. flippers; B. *three-sound words*: mill,

theme, rule; *four-sound words*: gruff, found, check;
five-sound words: trick, spring, clasp, wished, crisp; *six-
sound words*: plunk, strict, streets, lunged, splint

C.
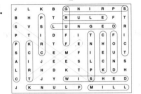

LESSON 3 B. Answers will vary. D. 1. last Saturday
2. Los Angeles 3. old rock tunes 4. four
5. guitar, keyboard, drums, and bass 6. they liked it
and cheered 7. drummer 8. they are the best rock
group that has ever played at Stone Park;
E. Answers will vary.

Chapter 7

LESSON 1 B. 1. Welcome 2. lemon 3. invite
4. chicken 5. pencil 6. gallon 7. kitten, orchard
8. travel 9. quarter 10. visit; C. Sunday, invite, Steven,
supper (2 times), lemon, chicken, soda, After, into,
apple (3 times), orchard, apples, filling, entire,
barrel, inside, gallons, cider, and seven should be
underlined.

LESSON 2 A. *sun*: sunflower, sunshine, Sunday,
sunlight; *snow*: snowplow, snowball, snowsuit,
snowflake; *rain*: raincoat, rainbow, raindrop; *-ball*:
snowball, softball, fireball; *-port*: airport, carport,
seaport; *-day*: Sunday, birthday, today; B. (Order of
answers will vary.) 1. butterfly 2. goodbye 3. rat-
tlesnake 4. understand; C. 1. underline snowsuit;
raincoat 2. underline raindrop; sunflower 3. underline snowball; softball 4. underline carport; seaport

LESSON 3 B. 1. unfair 2. unhappy 3. reread
4. disagree 5. rebuild; C. 1. unhappy 2. unpack
3. express 4. return 5. reread

LESSON 4 B. 1. *ful*: careful, hopeful, thankful,
harmful, thoughtful, painful, helpful, useful; *less*:
helpless, harmless, painless, thankless, careless,
hopeless, useless, thoughtless; *able*: honorable, sinkable, dependable, washable, reliable, breakable;
C. 1. helpful or useful 2. breakable 3. thankful
4. thoughtful, thoughtless, dependable or reliable
5. careful

LESSON 5 B. underline rain/coats, rain/drops,
rain/bows, butter/cups, sun/flowers, summer/time,
sea/shore, sea/shells, foot/ball, cheer/leaders,
winter/time, snow/flakes, snow/balls, and
snow/suits; C. Answers will vary. E. be/gin,
un/beat/a/ble, un/a/fraid, de/scribe, in/act/ive,
in/tol/er/ant, in/volved, in/ter/est/ed, a/ble,
re/li/a/ble, de/pend/a/ble, hon/or/able,
thank/ful, bash/ful, some/times, thought/ful,
help/ful, al/ways, fool/ish, child/ish, ad/mi/ra/ble,
qual/i/ties; F. Answers will vary.
G. Answers will vary.

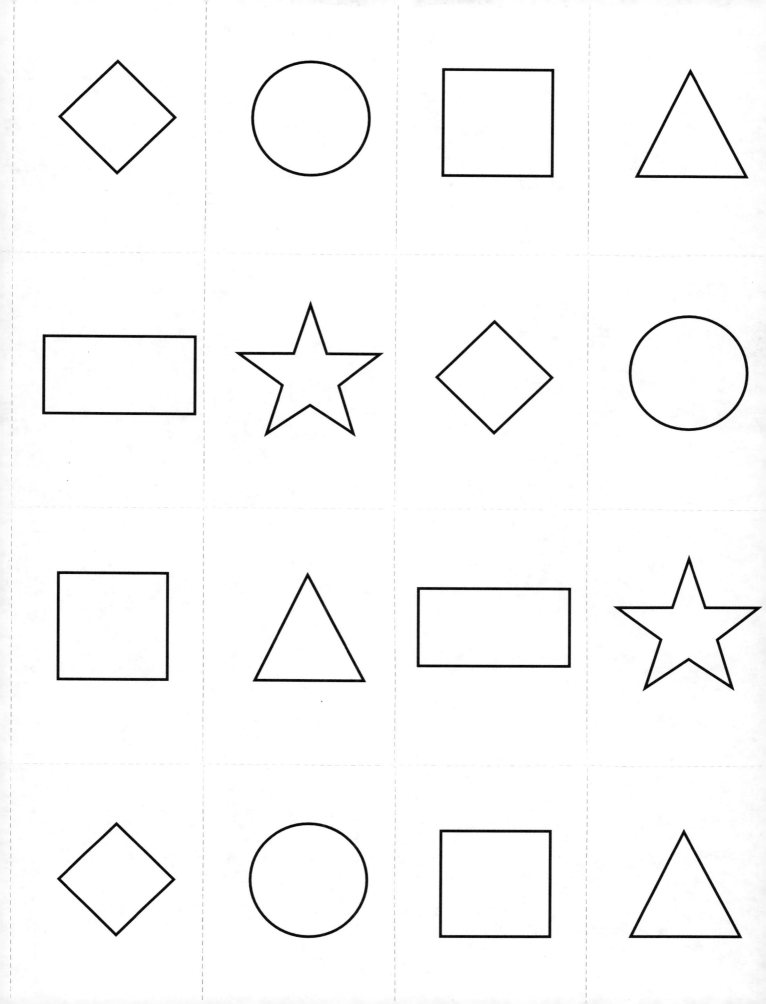

A	B	C	D
E	F	G	H
I	J	K	L
M	N	O	P

Q	R	S	T
U	V	W	X
Y	Z	a	b
c	d	e	f

g h i j

k l m n

o p q r

s t u v

w	x	y	z
a	b	c	d
e	f	g	h
i	j	k	l

m	n	o	p
q	r	s	t
u	v	w	x
y	z	ch	sh

th	wh	ai	au
aw	ay	ea	ee
ei	ey	ie	oa
oi	ou	ow	oy

ai	au	aw	ay
ea	ee	ei	ey
ie	oa	oi	ou
ow	oy	uy	ai